THE
BHAJAN

Christian Devotional Music
in the Indian Diaspora

H. JOY NORMAN

Published by

**MELROSE
BOOKS**

An Imprint of Melrose Press Limited
St Thomas Place, Ely
Cambridgeshire
CB7 4GG, UK
www.melrosebooks.com

FIRST EDITION

Copyright © H. Joy Norman, 2008

The Author asserts her moral right to
be identified as the author of this work

Cover designed by Sean Gladwell

ISBN 978-1-906050-51-1

Printed and bound in Great Britain by:
Biddles 24 Rollesby Road, Hardwick Industrial Estate
King's Lynn. Norfolk PE30 4LS:

To Kevin, Jonathan and Sunita

Errata

Page 32, line 1: She has found him

Page 36, line5: ...that singing *bhajans* helped...

Page 49, footnote 25: seat not heat

Page 94, line 1: Quote – "This species is...."

Page 112: delete Taize hymns under Music Example

Footnote 71: Note 78

Page 116, line 5: ...also indicated...

Contents

Contents (cont.)

Language and Orthography

As an English speaker, suggestions were made as to how one could communicate the Hindi terms without losing their meanings. Sympathetic Hindi speakers understood my predicament, as some of their friends and relatives spoke only English.

In this work, I have used Romanised Hindi words, which are italicised and juxtaposed with the equivalent English terms. I have kept as far as possible to the same spelling of a Hindi term, as there are variations in documents and texts.

List of Figures

List of Songs

List of Musical Examples

List of Photographs

Introduction

The story of the *bhajan* in its journey from East to West is about the way this South Asian devotional worship song for the assembly has developed in the Land of Bharat, as the sub-continent of Asia was called. It is about how South Asian and East Indian communities have attempted to maintain the form of this Hindu religious song, and moulded it and fused it into Christian hybrids.

Although the focus will be on England and Trinidad and Tobago, comparisons are inevitable with other areas where people from the sub-continent settled. After World War Two – with India's newly gained independence and Trinidad and Tobago's colonial status as a member of the British Commonwealth before its independence – India and Trinidad, the "Jewel in the Crown" and the "Crown Jewel"[1], were left to pursue their fortunes globally and as part of a diaspora.

The Indian Diaspora was no accident. Briefly, there are two strands: first, the continuing migrations of people from outside the Indian sub-continent over the centuries who settled there, and some of whose descendants migrated within the continent of Asia itself. In time, South Asian migrants from the continent of

---

1   Paul Scott's *Raj Quartet* describes some final difficulties in India's independence. *In* Crown Jewel, *Ralph De Boissiere writes of the birth pangs of Trinidad's independence.*

Asia, namely India, Pakistan and Bangladesh, made their homes in the North American, Australian and African continents, as they did in Great Britain and Europe. Second, the need in Great Britain for a new source of manual and agricultural labour for its colonies meant that it had to look elsewhere. Manual labour led to the building of the railways in Africa, and agricultural labour was needed for the sugar cane plantations in parts of that continent, as well as in the West Indies, Fiji and Mauritius.

The Emancipation Act of 1834 (introduced to Parliament by William Wilberforce) led to the abolition of slavery in the British Empire. Freedom meant that the slaves abandoned the sugar cane plantations, which would have been an economic near-disaster for some in Britain were it not for the import of a new labour force. London was appealed to by the planters and their managers, and it was to the Indian sub-continent that the governing authorities turned. The economic depression created by the British for the production of raw cotton in its home industry provided a ready source of migrant labour for the sugar cane industry. Slavery and indentureship were to mirror each other in terms of the standard of living, as the newcomers found to their detriment. Within this context, the Canadian Presbyterian Church and other Churches were prepared to help forge a better deal for the East Indian migrants. In Trinidad and Tobago, Mauritius and Fiji, in order to distinguish between the "new" immigrants and the indigenous peoples, the term "East Indians" was applied to the immigrants from India, as was also the case in Guyana in South America, and in other former British colonial lands.

The cultural trappings that accompanied the immigrants included language, dress, food and music, and, of course, religion. Where the artistic culture of religion is concerned, musical aspects of religious texts – melodies of prayers and chants – were orally transmitted, later written down and disseminated in print. These oral traditions were to change with time and place. This followed the pattern that had occurred so very long ago in the motherland. Cultures in ancient India were absorbed through interaction, and were conceived as a tangled web in which no one culture dominated throughout the centuries. Indeed, the sub-continent of India, Pakistan and Bangladesh was not as isolated from Europe as was first thought. Scholarly research points to discussions of philosophical doctrines between India and the Greek Empire in pre-Socratic times.[2]

By the fifteenth century, well-established poets of Hindu Bhaktism and Muslim Sufism coalesced in their rejection of caste and class. These poets came from humble beginnings. Their experience of social divisions was expressed in some of their poems. Bhaktism became a major cult within India's diverse communities and was perceived as a cohesive force for better relationships. Historically, it could also be viewed as a link between Ashoka, the Buddhist Emperor, and Akbar the Great, the Muslim Emperor.

In the third century BCE, Ashoka had continued the tradition of the Buddhist councils which tried to resolve religious and social conflict. High on the agenda of these discussions was a respect for opinions by and to all parties involved. This was no mean task, as the sub-continent of India stretched into what is now Afghanistan. Centuries later, Akbar the Great also attempted to resolve these divisions, and again it was an accepted condition that all discussion was carried on with a sense of propriety and respect. Sadly, today it appears that there is a great need by other such persons to assuage these conflicts before society completely disintegrates. Krishna's words, "I am become death, the destroyer of the worlds," would indeed be today's catastrophe.

It is perhaps to the literature of the great *Bhakti* poets that we

---

2　*Research is also being undertaken in the study of linguistics between ancient China (the Divine Land) and ancient India (the Celestial Store House).*

must look. In their Christian counterparts, these poets have left works which in the West are hardly known. They have married the emotion of Hindu Bhaktism with Christian doctrine. The works of these Indian Christian poets demonstrate that an Indian Church can be a continuum of a heritage of great diversity. The story of the *bhajan*, its history and its musical development, is also a story of transporting a culture.

The historical development of the *bhajan,* from Hinduism to its inculturation in Christian worship in the diaspora during the nineteenth century, was to have a great influence in the rites of the Roman Catholic Church and in the liturgies of the Church of South India and the Church of North India. Vatican II also acted as a catalyst to this end and was influential in imbuing Christian worship with a new musical ethos. It empowered the assembly – the people in congregations – to be directly responsible for their full participation in worship.

The issue of whether South Asian or East Indian communities have managed to retain their religious song as distinctly "Indian", and of what musical changes, if any, may have occurred through processes of assimilation, has been explored. What has been observed is the influence of societies and the impact of local culture on the music of the *bhajan.*

The traditions recollected by individuals are not only from those who lived in South Asian and East Indian communities, but also from those who grew up in these communities and moved away for different reasons – they moved to towns or abroad where job prospects and education were deemed better; emigration occurred during World War 2 to fill professional positions, especially in England and the Americas, and after the War to fill jobs rejected by residents in the host countries, and also as refugees from East Africa and elsewhere.

In this work, the symbolic, aesthetic and psychological features focus on people as well as on sound.

Acknowledgements

My thanks go to numerous persons who did not refuse me access to any part of their liturgical musical life. Their encouragement, and the information, which they shared with me was unselfish. A special thanks must go to Professor William (Bill) Tamblyn who introduced me to the subject of liturgical music for the assembly, and who initially supervised an earlier form of this work; to the library staff at Colchester Institute (a regional college of Anglia Polytechnic University), Richard Widdess of the School of Oriental and African Studies (SOAS), and Dr David Burnett formerly of All Nations' Christian College who advised me on some chapters, Dr Tina Ramnarine of Royal Holloway College, London University, who took a personal interest in my work, the late Bishop Leslie Brown, Rev. Robin Thomson and the staff and members of *South Asian Concern (SAC)*, Father Stephen Duncan in the USA, Gilda Sebastian (Asian Music Circuit) who has introduced South Asian Music to many audiences, and to Russ Pinder for the initial help in making the CD, and to Deaconess Lucy Ridsdale, Rev. Ivor Smith Cameroon, Rev. Andrew Davey and Mrs D. Sheriff.

Thanks to those who allowed me full access to their liturgical life: Rev. Paul Masih and the congregation of Calvary Church in Handsworth, Canon Bob Morris of St James, Handsworth, Amos Peters and the congregation of Good News Christian Church, Birmingham, Father John Wijngaards and Jackie Clackson of *Housetop*, London (who spent time singing their compositions to me), Rev. A.T. Mammen and Roy Thomas and the congregation of St John Mar Thoma Church in Hounslow, Deo Meghan, Paul Gazley of Truro Vineyard Christian Fellowship, and to the congregation of St John's Southall.

A special mention must go to Robinson Benjamin and his musicians for recordings by his group, and his translations of *bhajans* without which I would be lost, and to Chris Hale for his inspired performance. Thanks also to the participants in the first ever Indian sacred song competition in England, who kindly gave me permission to use their compositions – Hilary Brown, Chris and Doug Kekete, Palo Parkash, the Mowgli Group, Raj Kaul and Shaji Thomas.

From India: Rev. A. C. Oommen, Rev. Dr P. Kambar Manickam, principal of the Tamilnadu Theological Seminary, and to the many people to whom I spoke.

From Trinidad and Tobago: Dr Brinsley Samaroo of the University of the West Indies who read versions of this work, and patiently spent time informing me of historical facts; Rev. Teelucksingh, Indra Debysingh at St Andrew's Theological College library, Mrs Myrtle Sammy, Barry Mootoo of St Charles Church, Chaguanas, the Hindu Temple at Chaguanas, Lenore Mahase, Gail my sister-in-law for her recordings, Alan my brother for his support and endless information; to my dear father Leslie who kept on at me to "finish it" and continually supplied me with information and his recollections of events, and also to my dearest mother whose singing in Hindi was, in part, the inspiration for this subject.

Many of these persons have moved on to other places and careers since I first contacted them. If through negligence I have omitted any persons, I thank them now for their unselfish contributions.

Whatever the failings in this work where I had not addressed issues in detail, nor given weight where it is needed, it is due to my lack of the depth of perception in covering this subject, and not to any named persons or scholars mentioned; they have given me their time unstintingly, for which I am very grateful.

To the editorial team, thank you for your encouragement in publishing my manuscript, as I hope that it will inspire others to fill in the unknown gaps contained in this work.

In Nomine by John Taverner from *Early English Keyboard Music*, edited by Howard Ferguson. Oxford University Press 1971 & 1989. Reproduced by permission.

CHAPTER ONE

The Lord's Song in a Foreign Land
(Psalm 137:4)

For centuries the power of music in worship has been acknowledged by assemblies, who have effectively employed it to offer praise and inspire communities. "I will sing with my spirit," said Paul, "but I will also sing with my mind." It was a promise and a resolution, and within the context of I Corinthians 14:15 it was also in the act of worshipping together.

The universal Christian Church, representing all nations, is not tied exclusively to any race or nation; it is not tied to a particular way of life nor to any ancient or modern liturgical practices. As the Church professes to be able to commune with different forms of cultures, thereby enriching itself, it would appear to be consciously active in its universal mission. From its inception, the Christian Church expressed its new-found faith in song. The variety extends from chants and plainsong, through the harmonies of Bach to the evocative power of hymns, the strong rhythms of Gospel music, to a plethora of folk tune carols and world melodies and rhythms. Music in the Christian liturgy is

1

indispensable; its input is irreplaceable. As an integral element in worship, music has the capacity to aid in revealing central images of God, and the implications of these could be an advantage to the worshipping assembly. Music helps in the expression of faith, and the nourishment of that gift. However, it must also be recognised that Christian religious music is often assailed by tensions. In its failure to achieve a sense of balance and unity in a plurality of styles and forms, its antagonism to varying viewpoints frequently incites intolerance and opposition.

In order to oppose those negative views and stimulate the Church's growth in song – forms of the traditional and contemporary, the theoretical and practical, the aesthetic and the religious, the professional and the amateur – there needs to be respectful dialogue between the performer(s) and the participating assembly.

The Second Vatican Council (1962-65), or Vatican II as it is also called, ushered in an exciting renewal of worship within the Roman Catholic Church. Not since the Council of Trent (1545-63) had such an impact been made on the life of the Catholic Church. Trent was the most important ecumenical council between those of Nicea in 325 and Vatican II. There had been a demand by Catholics for a universal council following the spread of Protestantism. This Council was convoked by Pope Paul III, and dealt with the problems posed by the split in the Church. The Council met over three periods: 1545-47, 1551-52 and 1562-63. It defined Scripture and Tradition as two separate authorities, thus establishing a springboard for the renewal of discipline and spiritual life within the church. To help and encourage them with these important decisions, the work of Thomas Aquinas (1225-74) was studied.

Vatican II was convoked by Pope John XXIII. The life of the Church was examined by the Fathers of the Council. The past spiritual life and doctrine of the Church were analysed, and changes were made to the present forms of worship with an eye

2

to the future. To the astonishment of the Council members, the subject of music in worship was given a separate chapter which was almost the same length as that of the Eucharist. *The Instruction on Music in the Liturgy – "Musicam Sacram"* was issued on March 5, 1967 and included topics such as "Sacred Music in the Celebration of the Mass", "Language to be used in Sung Liturgical Celebrations", "Singing of the Divine Office", "Preparing Melodies for Vernacular Texts" and "Sacred Instrumental Music". There was also another chapter on "Music and Catholic Worship".

As recognised by Vatican II in the Consultation on the Sacred Liturgy, many cultures had different ways of expressing and creating their social identities through their music, where they employed various methods and styles of symbolising praise and sanctification within worship. It was acknowledged that the particular cultural context of a community needed to be considered as a primary force when assessing the participation of an assembly in its natural song and when evaluating the music in which they were engaged. For example, some cultures sang hymns from print, while other cultures used improvised call-and-response forms; both styles were accompanied or unaccompanied by instruments. Article 14 in the Constitution on the Sacred Liturgy addressed the public worship of the Church and considered the full participation of the worshipping assembly; praying in the mother tongue was more important than praying in Latin, the official language of the Catholic Church. Article 119 required the respect of local traditions and culture in countries where missionaries had been. However, to the dismay of many of these communities and those who ministered to them, instruments used in a secular setting were forbidden. Like a breath of fresh air, the proposals contained in the document were to have an effect on all denominations worldwide. Church people, the clergy as well as the laity, were challenged and encouraged to do their utmost to make the liturgy more relevant to the present and, above all, to be more meaningful to the people.

Vatican II established a firm foundation for the future of worship in the Christian Church. More importantly, it was also to free the Indian Christian Church from restrictions imposed on it by early Christian missionaries.

The Church in India was highly influenced by Western practices. In its architecture and political and social organisations, in services and in its music, and in its publications, Western forms and attitudes were prevalent[3]. There were experiments in areas such as architecture, Christian *ashrams* or religious communities, and in sacred music, where the use of "Christian lyric hymns in Indian metres sung to Indian tunes accompanied by Indian instruments" was imitated (Boyd, 1996:2). Socially, there had been Indian Christian poets and Indian Christian ascetic *sadhus* or holy men. Following the decrees of Vatican II the Church in India sought to make the liturgy more accessible to its assemblies. In India, where the cultures were more ancient than those of Europe, the use of vernacular languages, as well as the local genius of its peoples and their leaders, were harnessed by the presiding clergy. Local dress, musical instruments, music and architecture were adapted, thus forging a renewal of the worship life of the indigenous Church. These changes were approached through India's cultural heritage, its philosophy and theology.[4]

Historically, there was religious diversity in India, and it would be an error to assume that Indian history was Hindu history. The Vedas in the second millennium BCE, led the way to

---

3   *The complexity of cross-cultural missions between India and the West during the nineteenth and twentieth centuries presented some unusual twists and turns. Non-Christian Indians praised the missionaries for introducing Western science, medicine and technology. On the other hand, European Christians critised the Indian Church for being too Western and not maintaining indigenous cultural heritage. What both did not seem to recognise was their enthusiasms for something different which was a welcome change of tradition in their own cultures.*

4   *The author uses the term "India" to include Pakistan as well as Bangladesh as it was used before independence in 1947.*

Hinduism, a term used by the Persians and Arabs to indicate the landmass near the Sindhu or Indus River. Buddhism and Jainism had emerged by the sixth century BCE, Jews had settled in India after the fall of Jerusalem or even earlier, and later in waves during the fifth and sixth centuries and the eighteenth and nineteenth centuries. Christians were in Kerala in the fourth century, Parsees in the seventh century and the Baha'i refugees in the last century. Muslim Arab traders had sailed to India's western shores long before the invasions of other Muslims from the North West.

With this rich heritage, the Catholic Church, the Church of South India[5] and the Church of North India also took into account the various and rapid changes that were imminent in society and which had influence within their assemblies. Many efforts, some successful and some not as successful, were experimented with to make the Church "indigenous" in its life and worship.

Changes too were taking place in the Indian Diaspora as Christian worshippers began to explore their identity. Beside communication with the mother country, they turned to an historical wealth of Indian Christian lyrics which had accumulated in recent decades, and which acted as a bond between them. Some of these Christian poems expressed the thoughts and feelings of their authors, had the form and manner of songs, and many of them were intended for singing, not unlike the Psalms in the Old Testament.

One form of these lyrics, the *bhajan*, was an important item in Christian worship. This devotional worship song was to act as a force within immigrant groups from the sub-continent.

---

5 *The Church of South India (CSI) was created by the amalgamation of the main Protestant denominations. The inauguration took place in September 1947 at St George's Cathedral in Madras. It is said that a copy of the form of its liturgy was referred to by Vatican II Council.*

The Islands in the Indian Diaspora

Replacement of African slave labour by Indian indentureship took place across the British Empire, in the former colonies of Fiji, Mauritius, British Guiana, Trinidad and Tobago and other islands in the West Indies. The indenture system started at the end of slavery in 1834 and continued to 1920, when thousands of Indians were transported to the colonies to work in sugar cane plantations, as well as in other services in Natal, Burma (Myanmar), Ceylon (Sri Lanka) and Malaya. John Wear Burton (1875-1970), who was born in England but later emigrated to New Zealand, was asked to oversee the Indian missionary work in Fiji. He was appalled by the living conditions and exposed its abuses. His book, *Fiji of Today* (London 1910), led Rev. C.F. Andrews to agitate for the termination of the indentureship system. C. F. Andrews, who was a close confidant of Rabindranath Tagore and Gandhi, was concerned for bonded labourers in India and its colonies. He travelled especially to Fiji, Mauritius and Trinidad to see for himself the situations in which Indians from the subcontinent were employed[6]. He also travelled to Canada to see for himself how immigrants there had settled, and took up many causes on their behalf.

In Fiji missionaries had arrived via the Wesleyan mission in Tonga in 1835. In Mauritius, where the official language was French, the Roman Catholic Church was established. In 1856, Rev. Stephen Hobbs and Rev. Paul Ansorge were sent by the Church Missionary Society (CMS) to minister to the indentured workers.

In the West Indies, the second highest percentage of East Indians settled mainly in Trinidad, where Hindu and Muslim festivals were incorporated into the island's national calendar, one

---

6   *The focus here will be on Trinidad and Tobago. In terms of history and music, what has occurred there, where this devotional song acted as a force within the East Indian migrant groups, equally applies in Fiji and Mauritius as well as in Natal in South Africa and East African countries.*

ot these major festivals being Arrival Day. In this fête-orientated island, people of all religions joined together for fun before and after the serious business of worship. In the Indian communities, religious songs were all acknowledged as "godly songs" or "devotional songs" and included Hindu *bhajans*, Christian hymns, and Muslim *kaseeda*. Hindus pretended that there were no Muslim devotional songs, or that they were not familiar with them, yet they acknowledged the *quwaali* which was similar to the *bhajan*. In some villages of the diaspora where Hinduism was flourishing, devotees acknowledged Christian songs or hymns, whether they were choruses or spirituals. To many Hindus, Christ was a great yogi, and great delight was taken in singing a hymn such as "What a friend we have in Jesus". Hindu and Muslim pupils who attended Christian schools participated in prayers, read from the Bible and joined in singing hymns. They also attended church and took part in worship.

Rev. C.F. Andrews in Canada

7

In the West Indies the Roman Catholic and Anglican churches were established by colonists and administrators of the Crown. These two denominations ministered to the ruling classes and the ex-slave population, most of whom had moved to the towns. Like all the indentured immigrants to the British colonies, the recently arrived East Indian workers, or coolies, were subjects of enormous neglect because of language and religion, and sometimes they were designated pagans[7]. Accommodation was in barracks in which former slaves were housed. The barracks consisted of several small rooms in which families lived. The partitions were thin and did not reach to the ceiling, so there was no privacy. Cooking was done outside in front of the barracks; water was brought from streams or wells, and there were no toilet facilities. In Trinidad it was only on the arrival in 1868 of the Canadian missionaries from the Presbyterian Church, in the persons of Dr John Morton and his wife Sarah, that work was begun to improve the appalling social conditions in the East Indian communities. Morton's Hindi was good, unlike the Hindi spoken by the *sahibs*. He would read from the Hindi Bible when visiting various groups; he would explain certain passages, say prayers and sometimes sing a Christian *bhajan*. A printing press was set up, and this enabled him to print two editions of *Git Mala* or *A Garland of Songs,* which were *bhajans* and hymns compiled by him.

Throughout the diaspora, the discovery of appalling conditions in terms of housing, sanitation and education, which were imposed by the governing body and the planters, was slightly remedied. Missionaries made representations on behalf of the semi-enslaved East Indians, and it must have been after some time and constant nagging between parties that some relenting manifested itself, and the indentured labourers were allowed one free day away from the fields in order to perform some of their religious practices. Once

---

7   *In Trinidad approximately 144,000 immigrants arrived between 1847 and 1917.*

converted, they were given Sunday off. This made it possible for the missionaries to join in, in the few hours of relaxation and enjoyment which was the only time the workers got, to practice some of the customs of their homeland, like dancing and making music, besides, of course, the continuing use of their languages. The only way, therefore, the missionaries could have made any inroads into the lives of the labourers was through the vehicle of language. As a result of this, the missionaries may have conceived the idea of translating some words into Hindi for their own comprehension and satisfaction. Hindi then became the common language for all immigrants from the sub-continent.

Many of the East Indians were varied in their cultural and vocational skills. In the years following the Great Revolt (Indian Mutiny, 1857), now known as India's First War of Independence, there was an increase in the emigrations which had begun in 1845. Contrary to what was thought at the time, many of the arrivals were not mere peasants, but were artisans also seeking a new life in a new part of the world. So here were peasants, artisans, goldsmiths and silversmiths, soldiers who had taken part in the Revolt and were escaping the British Raj, conmen, business people who were debtors escaping the law, thieves and other enterprising souls bent on meeting with new changes and opportunities. A parallel can be seen in the matter of the Crusades, when the most motley group ever assembled under the banner of "Soldiers of the Cross", bent on opportunism, rapine and gains, got together to journey to the Holy Land.

Among these indentured labourers, there were some who had some form of education. These were chosen to assist the missionaries in translating and communicating to the others in their now common language of Hindi. At this stage, therefore, it can be assumed that the genesis for participation, exchange and fusion of both opposing sides came into play. What the missionaries did was to introduce some of their ideas – hymns, prayers and psalms –

which were translated into Hindi for the consumption of the masses, and indirectly introduced or imposed their forms of worship and Orders of Service in the other's camp, using the intellectual sector from the immigrant group to engage in transmission.

The name of Jesus was not anathema but rather a new dimension in the pantheon of gods (with their various *avatars* or reincarnations of Brahma, Vishnu, Rama, Krishna and others) in whom the immigrants had believed, and whom they were later to surrender for this Jesus. To the East Indians this gallery of gods was an important focus in a new situation, and among them accommodation was not possible; the newcomers contended that they had enough deities to seek solace with and to expect favours from.

The arrival of new groups of people into an already mixed society did nothing to enhance or add to the existing religious persuasions, but rather depended on the missionaries for their indulgence to change to another form of religious practice eventually operating under the guise of Christianity. The recently arrived immigrants in effect could add nothing new, but were rather the subjects for conversion and inclusion into the existing dispensation of the time. To the credit and possibly wily influence of the missionaries and their Indian assistants, some measure of infiltration manifested itself primarily through singing. Song and dance from the sub-continent also appeared to fill the need for something more substantial in terms of reassurance and security. Samaroo points to a more significant reason, in that migrant peoples, throughout history, have needed some reassurance in order to feel secure in their new-found countries; they therefore felt a need to identify with their culture before being allowed to adapt to a new one. For example, the importance of Israel to the Jewish Diaspora and that of the Emerald Isle to the American Irish (Samaroo, 1987:45-46).

In Trinidad and Tobago, during and after indentureship, many East Indian converts to Christianity who had moved into the towns joined the Anglican and Roman Catholic churches; however, the majority of converts came under the umbrella of Presbyterianism. Missionaries of the Canadian Presbyterian Church, later known as the Canadian Mission, who had been posted to the region had undergone training in India or had been trained in Indian thought in Canada before being sent to the West Indies. There followed a constant importation of Christian literature by the Presbyterians to Trinidad and Tobago. There was also the transfer of missionaries with experience in India to areas of the Caribbean and the other colonies. Indian religious thinking appears to have permeated Caribbean Presbyterianism so much that when the Susamachar Church, or Church of Glad Tidings, was being built, a sacred pipal tree[8] was brought from India and planted next to the church.

Pipal tree and Susamachar Church – Trinidad (HJN)

Missionaries introduced many Christian *bhajans* which they had learnt in India; some also trained in Canada, and Western hymns were translated into Hindi for the benefit of their future

---

8 *According to Hindu mythology the pipal tree was the abode of the gods.*

congregations. As a result, there was in the Presbyterian churches – and in worship at other venues – a programme in which English, as well as Canadian and American hymns, and Indian Christian *bhajans* were sung.

An early practice actively employed was *bhajan* singing at evenings after work, more so at weekends when the brief respite from the sweltering heat of the cane fields served as a form of therapy[9].

> Labourers assembled at a hut with their musical instruments
> and chanted bhajans, livening up the gatherings with fun and
> jokes with much laughter and hilarity as a relief from tasks
> in the fields and free from all manner of supervision[10].

In the church service, the singing of a *bhajan* was an important item.

Figure 1: *Order of Service*

Opening Prayer
Hymn
Bible Reading / Psalm
Offering
Sermon
Bhajan
Prayer or Mizah[11] Benediction
Announcements
Closing Prayer/Benediction

---

9 *This form can be equated with the plight of the slaves who had their form of diversion in the spirituals.*

10 *The author has drawn on the collective memories of people and communities in the countries cited in this work. This collective memory links the past with the present, and has a bearing on the future. It is a way of explaining distant characteristics of the South Asian traditions, and is a key for the understanding of the development of the bhajan and its journey throughout the Indian diaspora.*

11 *Thanksgiving*

It is remembered as being integral to the service for the following reasons:

1. Some of the very old folk who were not literate in the English words of the hymns were accommodated by having one of the hymns sung in Hindi, as well as the inclusion of a *bhajan*;

2. Some of the young people were desirous of learning something of their relatives' past and their indulgence in worship, and so also joined in singing the *bhajan*;

3. The inclusion of one *bhajan* in the service was a necessary means of retaining the church attendance of older people who, in the main, comprised the majority of worshippers;

4. It was some time later, after a short period of its absence, when there seems to be a resurgence in the younger people for a knowledge of Hindi, that *bhajans* with Hindi words were translated into English for the younger voices who found some relish in singing them.

Bhajans were also sung to celebrate the public holiday of Arrival Day. A Service of Thanksgiving was held to commemorate the anniversary of the arrival of East Indians to Trinidad:

Presbyterian women dressed in their saris and shalwars seemed to embrace the spirit of the occasion, which was one of joyful celebration and affirmation of identity. The service included singing of *bhajans* by the congregation … The sounds of *dholaks, dhantals*, and chac chacs filled the Susumachar Church and added to the mood of celebration.   (*The Trinidad Presbyterian*, July 1995:1)

At funerals, the deceased might have requested that at his departing this life, a *bhajan* should be sung. The ritual of funerals was brought to the islands of the diaspora, and drumming and instrumental accompaniment to the singing of *bhajans* continued for twenty days. *Bhajans* sung in the Christian context were accompanied by clapping, and it could be assumed that *bhajans* from Hinduism were also sung, as relatives of the deceased, who had retained their Hindu faith, would have requested their inclusion.

Bhajans were also taught at schools, but in Hindi, and many children did not understand what they were singing:

> It was most undesirable for most of us who could not understand one word of Hindi, plus the fact that none of the teachers thought it necessary to translate for us what the words meant.

As well as being an integral item in the church service, *bhajans* were also enjoyed and performed as part of the cultural activities of the people:

> I remember with some degree of surprise, my wedding entourage being welcomed at your Nana's [maternal grandfather] with some *bhajan* singing; and on this occasion of leaving with Mama, some sad dirges were sung with much crying from the women, representing or indicating a sadness associated with the new life of the bride into another family, and wishing for a happy absorption and acceptance on the next side and the newer community.

There were some Presbyterian churches where no *bhajans* were sung, as there were none of the older folk still alive to lead the singing. It could be assumed that there may have been a psychological response of not singing *bhajans,* as in doing so would demonstrably negate one's standing of being "Western" in a plural society. This indeed was the case in the main towns.

Christian *bhajans* were also introduced by immigrants who later came to the island. There were some who had already been converted to Christianity in India:

> Unlike many Indian people who were converted to
> Christianity in Trinidad, many indentured labourers were
> already Christians in India ... some came with names like
> James or John.

Immigration records show no evidence of early indentured labourers using Christian names, and these names only emerged when the later waves of immigrants had settled in securely. Some of these immigrants apparently concealed their Christian names so as to mix freely with Hindus and Muslims on board ship. Christianity was seen as the religion of the ruling British Raj.

Christian *bhajans* were also introduced to Trinidad and Tobago by Indian Christian missionaries. The Presbyterian missionaries were finding it difficult to meet the challenge of both Hindu and Muslim missionaries from India, and therefore a Christian Indian missionary was invited to attempt to restrain Trinidad Indians from returning to their original faiths.

Communication in Hindi and the singing of the *bhajans* bridged the chasm between communicated and communicator and established the formation of a kind of common ground. The singing and chanting of Hindu *bhajans* with the accompaniment of clapping of hands and the shaking of heads from side to side, were transferred to the singing of Christian *bhajans*. It can be deduced that the missionaries captured this same scenario and transformed it by transplanting their words in Hindi with the lively tunes, but with the Christian mutation in meaning. Instead of singing to their God, which they claimed was the one and same God of us all, but which assumed different incarnations (Vishnu, Ram, Siva, Indra etc.), and numerous others who constituted their pantheon of gods and this apotheosis, the Christian community instituted the idea of God as being mainly represented in the person of Jesus Christ, Lord. In effect, this mutation from singing Hindu *bhajans* to Christian ones involved only a change of words, designed not to disturb the trend of singing or make any drastic changes which would have discouraged participation or indulgence as some new presentation, which would have been unacceptable. In time, the missionaries were able to slip in more dogma or doctrine now that common ground was established, as the converts were becoming more amenable to listening and change.

A notable aspect of worship for the assembly was the special format according to which it was conducted. Many of the older generations remembered that the service began with a prayer, followed by an invocation, the singing of *bhajans*, readings from the sacred book, the *Bhagavad Gita*, equated with the Bible, explanations and sermon as equated with the sermon. The worship then closed with more *bhajans* and prayers followed by a benediction. All in all there seems to have been a liturgy already in effect, but according to Hindu tradition; this was modified in order to absorb the Christian doctrine and theology, and pave the way more easily towards conversion. As a result of this, those who accepted Christ were schooled, educated and employed in small missions and centres, thus removing them from the ignominy of labouring in the fields, which only served to dehumanise their persons. The result of this was the commencement of the integration process into the form of worship in gatherings, which later became churches, and with the singing of hymns translated into Hindi for the comprehension of the congregation.

From this situation there were to emerge young men, and soon after, women, who would become catechumens and ministers in the churches throughout these islands of the Indian diaspora.

Great Britain

During the seventeenth century, South Asians began to appear in London, as a result of the establishment of the East India Company. The capital had been a magnetic centre for immigrants and refugees of different nationalities over the centuries. Many of the first South Asians were brought to England in private households, and when their services were no longer required they were left to fend for themselves on the streets. During both World Wars many Indians from the sub-continent and the diaspora served in professional capacities and in other jobs.

Figure 2: *The Indian Diaspora*

Burma	Netherlands
Canada	Sri Lanka
East & Central Africa	South Africa
Fiji	Singapore
Gulf	Surinam
Guyana	Trinidad & The Caribbean
Malaysia	Great Britain
	USA

In later years there was an influx from the Caribbean, East Africa and countries of the Indian diaspora. A small number came from South East Asia, such as Fiji, Singapore and Malaysia. Many of these immigrants, especially Hindus, settled where former immigrants had settled, or where their languages were spoken – Gujarati, Punjabi, Hindi or Tamil. Many settled along what was known as the Asian Corridor of England, from Southampton and London to Leicester, Coventry, Wolverhampton and Birmingham, to Leeds and further, in Scotland and later Northern Ireland. The arrival of these new immigrants – Buddhists, Jains, Muslims, Sikhs and Hindus – brought a new dimension to Britain.

Historically, this island was a sea-faring nation, and a multi-ethnic society, as immigrants had been motivated by pull factors, such as the demand for labour, and push factors, such as the need to escape religious persecution. From the second part of this statement it is apparent that a certain degree of religious tolerance was in place. However, the Christian churches, which were offered an unexpected opportunity for renewal due to this new influx, failed to grasp this. It was a sad indictment of mainline churches; a dialogue of inter-faith conventions was as far as some groups could envisage. The churches were in for a bumpy ride, and many looked for ways in which to penetrate this shifting society by amassing and assessing a variety of intellectual, organisational and liturgical forms. It was a beginning. From a Protestant point of view, this created an amorphous mass of chatter and clatter. Suddenly, in order to be "modern" and tolerant and intellectual, theological and moral debates were initiated by well-meaning bodies. There was the reorganization of parishes, priests and people; there was the modernising of the liturgy, and new translations of the Bible and the Prayer Book. Ecumenically, there was greater ecclesiastical collaboration through the Anglican-Methodist Unity Scheme. The Churches Together movement was also established in towns and cities, and this consisted of all Christian denominations. The most important ecclesiastical event, which was to have a remarkable effect on the character of all Christendom, was Vatican II. On a global scale, for Protestants and Catholics, the ripples were penetrating; on its own, it created a momentum in which discussion and change were quickly put into practice.

In England the South Asian community was not static, nor is it today. It became a homogeneous community. It was, and is now even more so, very diverse, changing frequently as new generations grow up. It is to be expected that complexities in inner cities with high-density populations are not the same as those in the suburbs or rural areas. The presence of large numbers of people in this country "of Hindu, Sikh and Muslim backgrounds is a challenge that the church has had to face over the past years" (Root, 1998:70). Many Christian Indians, for whom the English language presented no difficulty, felt that they had been sidelined by mainstream churches and did not feel welcome. Although some Asians attended services or mass at the local church in the morning, they and the majority of Christian Asians also attended an afternoon service, which was packed and which was specifically Asian-oriented in language with some English[12]. A local church building of a Christian denomination was "borrowed" between services or after the evening service, as was the cathedral in Birmingham after evensong. Other Christian Asians acquired a building or a disused church for their worship, where services were held in a specific language or multi-Indian languages. Another initiative was the numerous conventions where Christian Asians met socially and worshipped together.

Although some churches had made great attempts to accommodate the Christian immigrants as well as British Asians born here, some worshippers felt that they had not been taken seriously and played no part in the churches' elected councils[13]. (Fortunately, this has now been rectified, as seen in the number of minorities in leading positions.) However, for the majority of Asians, Christianity was still seen as part of Western culture, and many questioned whether the churches in England were ready to receive "new" believers from other faith and cultural backgrounds which, in the long run, would have enriched the liturgies. Meanwhile, some Asian individuals and families went straight into the structures of an average "English culture" church and found it satisfactory. A resulting factor, due to a flux of conflict, was the formation of Asian Independent Fellowship groups which began to flourish in the seventies within the established Anglican, Methodist, Presbyterian and Baptist structures. These became increasingly culturally independent but also mingled with evangelical and Pentecostal elements. Due also to the negative

---

12 *I attended such a service in Handsworth, Birmingham, where there were over 200 worshippers. I also was present at others, where for my benefit, the pastor/preacher also spoke in English, as well as in the Indian languages of the congregation.*

13 *See Deo Meghan's research on the makeup of committees for the Minority Ethnic Anglican Concerns, Crowther Hall, Birmingham.*

attitude often experienced, a thriving outreach programme from Christian Asians to non-Christian Asians was established through some local churches, *satsangs* or truth gatherings, other social groups, clubs and conventions. There was also a focus on community needs, such as the teaching of English and learning about the British way of life in a socio-political context.

An insight into the mission work of some of these groups is to be seen in three towns, although many more exist. Since 1981, the Derby Asian Christian Ministry Partnership (DACMP) has aimed to reach Asians in the city where churches were created and where people of all races would feel at home and flourish. This project involved fifteen churches of different denominations with Asian, Black and European members; there was a monthly multicultural service that was hosted by a different church each month. In Hounslow, West London, a significant part of the work was the focus on the younger Asian generation who were born in England and who had been brought up there, and found themselves caught between two cultures. Within the United Kingdom, new Christians were often from the younger generation and were accused of rebelling against their own culture:

> When I was baptised, my church wanted me to change my name to an English name ... I told them my name, Jayesh, meant "victorious one" and didn't see that God would want me to change.

The local churches catered for a range of activities, including children's clubs, toddlers' groups and language groups. There was also fellowship/inter-church ministry which encouraged and co-ordinated culturally sensitive evangelical work in the area; and there was also training which encouraged Christians in all aspects of life. In Leicester, the ministry was aimed at reaching Gujaratis and Punjabis and included two Bible study groups, one of which was church based and intended for Christians; the second was evangelistic and was based around home visits. The leaders encouraged integration into the community through church co-operation and social events.

In the global spectrum, although Britain forms the heart of the South Asian community in Europe, there are significant communities in Europe where business opportunities have presented themselves[14]. Many South Asians who arrived in England from East Africa and other parts of the world emigrated to Paris, Geneva, Lisbon or Moscow if the pay was right and the opportunities for business existed. At a conference held in the Netherlands at the end of 2006, Christian South Asians and European Christians gathered to worship and to pray together, and to share information. What was interesting was the participation of Christian missionaries from Kerala, Sri Lanka, Bhutan and India.

It appears that North America, however, is replacing the United Kingdom as the largest South Asian community:

> When I arrived in New York, I just opened the phone book, found someone with my surname and called them and went and stayed with them.

> I have ten years left before I retire. If I go to America, I can earn four times more what I earn in the UK. I want my last ten years to really count.

Cities such as Toronto, New York, Los Angeles, Chicago and San Francisco all account for large communities of South Asians.

In these countries, music played an important part and was considered an integral facet in the Asian network. In the convention of *Asia Celebrates Jesus Christ 2000,* and subsequent conferences, thousands of Asian Christians gathered to worship. Here traditional Western hymns and worship songs were easily amalgamated with those of the East. The celebration, the largest of its kind, came after a rapid growth in the number of Asian

---

14 How many South Asians in Europe? *Thomas Hieber has compiled resources and information (January 2007). Thomas.Hieber@gmx.net.*

Christians in Britain over the past three decades.

In the contemporary scene, where Asian pop groups were and are leading the field and creating new sounds, so also in Christian worship a number of people began to experiment with different musical forms. This has been evident in the combined use of both Western and Indian instruments. Some Christian groups play and sing in both Western and Asian styles; others are developing a multi-cultural fusion, and even rap and other creative forms are being experimented with. Some link to a very specific tradition; for example, Gujarati Hindu devotional music.

Not only are British Asians forging ahead in using music as a means of communicating the Gospel, other worship leaders, including the traditional clergy, are beginning to attempt to meet the needs of their multi-ethnic assemblies and are composing new worship songs. Where the *bhajan* is concerned in Christian worship in England, although the basic form is mostly employed in *satsangs*, house groups and other venues, some variations have evolved and are used frequently. In many respects it is an attempt by Asian Christians in England and further afield to worship in diverse ways, without forgetting their individual cultures, but also integrating into a culture already enriched over many centuries.

CHAPTER TWO

The *Bhajan* in Hinduism
The *Bhakti* Movement

The *Bhakti* movement in Hinduism acted as a catalyst to music. Hinduism was a growing and mobile religion in the sub-continent, and the *Bhakti* sect was part of this development. Music for worship, therefore, followed the contemporary developing trends. In its early sacred music, the Brahmin priests chanted in Sanskrit. This was to change when the leaders and *sants* or saints within the *Bhakti* movement chose song as a medium for the propagation of their thoughts and messages, which stressed the need for virtuous living. No longer was the role of a priest essential. The movement gave rise to a musical form of the *bhajan*, which was later to be adopted by churches in India.

The *Bhakti* movement in India was responsible for the spread of Vaisnavism, which was the most popular form of Hindu theism centered on the worship of Vishnu, one of the *trimurti* or triad comprising Brahma, Vishnu and Siva. Devotees of Vishnu also worshipped his *avatars* or reincarnations, which were celebrated in the Puranas written in Sanskrit, the most famous of which was the *Bhagavata Purana* (c. 900). This was composed in the Tamil country of South India, where the worship of Vishnu had been introduced from the north. The Alvars or poet-saints were Tamil singers who composed numerous hymns which appealed to the masses, and who flourished about the middle of the eighth century to the middle of the ninth century. These Alvar compositions, which incorporated music, dance and singing, inspired many poets to write lyrics in several Indian languages. These poems soon spread to the North, together with the teachings of other holy men. Hawley relates the dissemination of these lyrics in a description of the Sanskrit scriptures as "a lovely woman who was born in the south (about the sixth century AD), gained strength and maturity in the middle regions of the West (from the twelfth century onward), grew old, and was revived to experience her full flowering when she reached the north." (1988:6).

The lyrics of the *bhajans* were marked by a fervent devotion to Krishna, and were introduced into the worship of the Sri-Vaisnava temples in the south by Brahmin migrants. An analogy may be drawn between the religious literature in England during the thirteenth century and that of the literature in India. Themes of divine love in Latin hymnology, which were adopted by European and British poets, expressed the yearning of the human soul for union with the divine. Many of these religious Latin lyrics, with their devotion to the Blessed Virgin and love of Jesus, were later translated into the vernaculars.

The *Bhakti* cult, which originated in the Dravida country, flourished in Karnataka, had some success in Maharashtra, but was not so successful in Gujarat[15]. The *Gita Govinda* of Jayadeva, who lived in the thirteenth century in Orissa, had been a unique

---

15 *The term "cult" in this context means to cultivate, to worship, to care. In Christianity, Thomas Aquinas gave it a precise meaning for scholarly use in the whole system of religious belief and ritual.*

phenomenon in Indian music, and was one of the finest products of the *Bhakti* movement. This became the main inspiration of a flowering musical dance-drama all over East and South India, where it fostered the *keetan* and *bhajan* musical dance-drama traditions. The *Bhakti* cult also laid a foundation for composite Indian culture and derived the best from both Hindu and Islamic cultures. Sufi saints adopted the *Bhakti* ritual through the influence of the Hindu *Bhakti* cult. Muslim *fakirs* ranked with Hindu *sants*, like Tukaram and Eknath, who sang in both Hindi and Urdu. Notable *sants* in the *Bhakti* movement – such as Kabir, Tulsidas, Ravidas, and the *bhaktas* Nanak, Surdas and Mirabai – preached and composed in local languages, rejected all kinds of caste distinctions, condemned rituals and encouraged community singing or *kirtana,* which became popular. Although these *sants* were divided in their thinking – the Catholics, so to speak, and the Protestants – they were all part of an increasing collective group spear-heading the *Bhakti* movement over a millennium period throughout India. "The poems of these holy people stand at the fount of the Hindi language" (Hawley 1988:4), and unlike the poems in England of Milton and Donne, these verses are quoted by, and are familiar to, any schoolchild and the ordinary man in the street; they are not unlike Aesop's Fables or some quotations from Proverbs in the Old Testament. They were, and are today, kept alive by the singing and the recitations of peripatetic "troubadours" who visit villages. Although the verses are religious in context, they describe the trials of life, "the hollow shell of the body", friendship, betrayal, death and love.

These poets, although referred to as *bhakti* poets, are also described as *sants*. A *sant* was seen as someone who was true or good, as well as someone who incarnates what is life. The English word saint may be applicable in this context, just as the term *bhakta*, devotee or lover of God, may be also used in an honorific sense. The terms *sant* and *bhakta* did not indicate any theological learning, but indicated the two strands in the *bhakti* genre. The *sants* preferred to worship God without attributes or form, and had no inclination to worship through icons. The *bhaktas* were of the opinion that God took on forms of some description; for example, an image in the temple or as a character in history to guide people. Thus the two schools of belief, the *nirguna*, without attributes or form, and the *saguna* with attributes, existed side by side.

The six highly individual poets and their followers were united in their personal experience in religion but were not attached to any organisation. They were very critical of the Brahmins and the conceit of the caste system. To them the use of the Sanskrit language was anathema in communicating their thoughts to their followers and the ordinary people whom they met on their travels. (It was a scenario similar to that of the use of Latin in the Roman Catholic Church.) In order to disseminate their personal religious thought in poetry, they adopted the vernacular languages of the people with whom they came in contact. The role of the priest was thus negated. The *bhakti* poems, which emphasised strong individual traits, were composed in a petitionary style called *vinaya* or "humble submission". The result of this genre made it feasible for these poems to be brought together in anthologies.

The Nirguna Saints

The three *nirguna* saints, Ravidas, Kabir and Nanak, believed that God did not exist in any shape or form; he exceeded or was beyond the shapes which human senses perceive in the world, and therefore no iconic means were necessary. To grasp the truth was to do so through one's heart and soul, and through a sense of faith.

Ravidas of Benares, who lived in the fifteenth or sixteenth century, today is acknowledged as the great Untouchable saint of North India. He was a *chamar*, a shoemaker, who worked with the hides of dead animals; this trade, as Ravidas was well aware, was considered the lowliest of the lowly:

> Oh well born of Benares ... my labour is with leather.
> ... And I, born among those who carry carion
> in daily rounds around Benares, am now
> the lowly ones to whom the mighty Brahims come ...[16]

As one of the *bhakti* poets he is held in high esteem by Hindus of all backgrounds. In his poetry Ravidas indicates fellow poets with whom he associated, or whom he followed in the hierarchical structure:

> ... And he has exalted Namdev and Kabir,
> Tricolan, Sadhna, and Sen.
> Listen saints, says Ravidas,
> Hari accomplishes everything.

Hagiographical tradition mentions that Mirabai, another *bhakti* saint, is said to have travelled from Rajasthan to meet Ravidas, as told in the *Ravidas Ramayana*. Other stories include the meetings of the renowned yogi Gorakhnath and the Brahmin Ramanand. Ravidas' *bhakti* poems appear to raise social issues concerning caste in Hinduism:

> A family that has a true follower of the Lord
> Is neither high caste nor low caste, lordly or poor.

His influence lingered long after his death and the building of a temple in Sri Govardhanpur near the Benaras Hindu University is still a beacon for pilgrims. It stands as a rival to other temples, as it was built for the lower castes who are not always welcome in the city's other temples.

Kabir could be compared to Amos or Jeremiah, the prophets of the Old Testament, in that he was likely to be at odds with the world in which he lived. Kabir was a weaver (*julaha, kori*), which

---

16 *The following quotes are by Hawley unless otherwise stated.*

was a low caste, and had every reason to turn to Islam. Although his name is a Muslim one, a Quranic form of Allah, "great", he criticised both the Muslim and Hindu religions:

> Hindus, Muslims – where did they come from?
> Who got them started down this road?

This could hardly have endeared him to the Muslim *qazis* who expounded the Muslim law in mosques or at courts ruled by Turkish ancestry, nor by the arrogant Brahmins. Nevertheless, his proverbs were quoted frequently by the ordinary people:

> If caste was what the Creator had in mind,
> why wasn't anyone born
> with Siva's three-lined sign?

> If you're a Brahmin,
> from a Brahmin woman born,
> why didn't you come out some special way?

> And if you are a Muslim,
> from a Muslim woman born
> why weren't you circumcised inside?

In the poetry of Kabir, who became an honoured *sant* and poet in the fifteenth century, there is a synthesis of the best from Islam and Hinduism:

> If the mosque is the place where God resides,
> then who owns the rest of the land?
> Ram lives in images and holy locations?
> Then why has no one ever found him there?

In Kabir's thoughts, God could not be named, described or held.

Nanak the Teacher, Nanak the Preceptor, is the one North Indian saint to whom a religious society is linked and is identifiable by his pupils, the Sikhs. Nanak was born in Rai Bhoi di Talvandi (now called Nankana Sahib in his honour) near Lahore in 1469. His father was a *bedi khatri*, a member of the merchant caste. After the death of Nanak in 1539, the Sikh community established specific rituals and festival days, identified a place of pilgrimage, Goindval, then later Amritsar, where the Golden Temple was built.

The Golden Temple in Amritsar (HJN)

The *Adi Granth* was their authoritative canon, and it is from the first two emblems of this book that the words attributed to Nanak emerged, *ek omkar* – "I Omkar" or simply "I OM." It signified that God is One, OM. Of all the *bhakti* poets Nanak believed that one had to wait patiently and silently for the divine truth:

> From listening,
> sin and sorrow
> disappear.

Nanak preached God's total truth, man's inability to capture it, and the order which emanated from a transcendental state. Nanak's teaching provided his followers with a perception of divine power, with them being instrumental to God's plan. He taught through the medium of poetry, and one of his main themes was the Word, or Name, of God. According to Nanak, the Word *(sabd)* is the real guru who dispenses order and blessing. The remembrance, love, and most of all the repetition of the Name, negates all human self-centredness. The Name is an ocean, which encompasses all the divine as being motionless and immovable *(acal)*, without any beginning *(anadi)*, timeless *(akal)*, colourless *(anil)*, spotless *(niranjal)*, unborn *(ayoni)*, intangible *(achut)*, indestructible *(anahat)* and other names.

In the Sikh *gurudvara*, temple, the vernacular Word is paramount; people come to hear the Book being read at any hour of the day. As a congregation, worshippers think, listen together and sing. In the *gurudvara* there is an air of quietness as the reader *(granthi)* cares for the Book and the three cantors *(ragis)* lead the attendees in singing the poems from the *Adi Granth*. Nanak proposed that by listening, by pondering and by singing, worshippers achieved a sense of positive wellbeing:

> From listening,
> a depth, a well of virtues;
>
> Nanak says,
> those who hear,
> flower forever.
> *(Japji 11)*

The Saguna Saints

The *saguna* saints, Surdas (Sur), Tulsidas (Tulsi) and Mirabai (Mira), were devotees who were identified with one personal form of God; for Surdas and Mirabai this was Krishna, and Tulsidas was associated with Ram. The *saguna* poets advocated that what people could see, what was tangible, had a steadying influence on them; it helped in concentration in worship.

Surdas (1483-1573). Nothing is really known about Sur's life, except that which is attributed to Gokulnath's *Caurasi Vaisnamvan ki Varta* and the accompanying commentary by Hariray. Both Gokulnath (traditionally 1551-1640) and Hariray (impressive lifespan, 1590-1715) were important figures in the descending line of the sixteenth century theologian Vallabhacarya (Vallabha). Vallabha inculcated in his disciples a sense of devotion to Krishna as a child and youth. The eight-period ritual of the day emphasised the earthly life of Krishna and its yearly celebrations. Just as the festivals of the liturgical Christian calendar provided subjects for religious lyrics, so did the Hindu festivals inspire the *Bhakti* poets. Surdas was noted for his descriptions of the child Krishna and the tender parental emotions they conveyed. In the following poem, Krishna (Gopal) is addressed by Yasoda, his foster mother, who tries to convince him to drink milk from a black cow, which will make his black hair grow longer; she also prepares him for future battles in his childhood and in his adolesence with the usurper king of Mathura and Kesi a demonic horse.

> If you drink the milk of the black cow, Gopal,
> You'll see your black braid grow.
> … So drink: the fires daily burn in the bellies
> of your foes – Kans and Kesi and the crane
> … Sur says, Yasoda looks at his face and laughs
> when he tries to coax his curls beyond his ear.

Other poems describe the amorous escapades of Krishna, which are seen through the eyes of the *gopi* or milkmaid, and which is projected through the persona of Surdas. In this poem Sur depicts Radha's reaction to Krishna; in it the intensity of love is celebrated by the lover who longs for the beloved, not only when he is absent but also when he is present:

She's found him, she has, but Radha disbelieves
That it's true, what she sees when her eyes behold
her master's moonlike face.
Her gaze is fixed, but her mind is glazed;
her eyes refuse to close;
And her intellect wages a ranging debate:
Is it a dream? Or is this her true Lord?
Her eyes fill and fill with beauty's high pleasure,
then hide it away in her breast:
Like bees driven wild by any distance from honey
they dart back and forth from the hoard to the source.
Sometimes she musters her thoughts; she wonders:
"Who does he love? Who can this Hari be?"
For love, says Sur, is an awkward thing.
It ripples the mind with waves.

Surdas was blind, and this handicap was said to have given him a unique "insight" to the divine world. The legacy he has left in India, besides his poems, is his name; many blind people adopt his name as a mark of respect, which is shown to them and to Surdas.

Mirabai (1498-1576) is the only female poet of north India who became famous[17]. Her counterpart in South India was Antal of the Alvar poet saints. Mira can be equated to Saint Teresa in her religious ecstacies, and her poems of divine love are like those of the English poet, Crashaw. Her divine infatuation was the cause of much strife in her personal life. Like Kabir, Mirabai's songs are sung all over India, even by those whose language is not Hindi. For one so important, only two poems with Mirabai's aural signature exist, one of which is in the Adi Granth. It is very

---

17 *Male poets assumed female personae in order to express the intense*
   emotion that they assumed to be those of a woman. To impersonate a
   woman, these male poets had to work hard to interpret and experience
   God as lover and husband (it could be compared to the figure of the bride
   of Christ in Christian theology, or the ecstasies of Theresa of Avila).
   Mirabai, as a woman from Rajasthan, could fully indulge herself as a
   devotee, lover and husband to Krishna, as well as a gopi.

likely that, as a woman, her poems were excluded from devotional anthologies. Her songs and poems, however, were performed by travelling bards or groups. Tradition has it that Emperor Akbar (1562-1605) risked his life by entering a Hindu enclave during a period of political unrest to hear her sing; he was accompanied by the famous singer of his court, Tansen. The hagiography of Mirabai alludes to her being a princess, and a stubborn one at that, who refused to bow her head to her mother-in-law as well as the chosen household god. To do so would have been a betrayal of her lord, Krishna, as her emotional *bhakti* poems inclined towards her devotion to him.

Bhakti as a force propels a person beyond reasonable confines, as when Surdas takes on the voice of a *gopi*. To Mirabai as a woman, the boundary to which she was propelled was that of marriage to the world's most eligible, and most unmarriageable, bachelor, and this was seen as madness in the Hindu world:

> Sister, I had a dream that I wed
> the Lord of those who live in need:
> Five hundred and sixty thousand people came
> and the Lord of Braj was the groom.
>
> In a dream they set up a wedding arch;
> in a dream he grasped my hand;
> in a dream he led me round the wedding fire and I became
>   unshakably his bride.
> Mira's been given her mountain-lifting Lord:
> from living past lives, a prize.

Many themes in Mira's poetry emphasise the importance of the name of God; she praises the true Guru and uses nautical imagery to "cross the sea of existence", and believes strongly in being in company with other worshippers, *sants*, *sadhus* and *bhaktas*. A distinct trait in her poems, and not in the poems of other *bhakti* saints, is the style in which her aural signature is given. It is integral to the phrase or line. In other *bhakti* poems, the names of the poets can be omitted from the text which then becomes anonymous; for example, in poems by Ravidas and Kabir, the signature is stated as "says Kabir" or "Ravidas says". It may also be understood, as in the case of Nanak and Sur, only the name appears, and the listener or reader can supply the verb "says". In the poems of Mira, the poet is part of the whole poem – the whole phrase becomes her signature:

> You are the Lord who cares for the fallen;
>   rescue whoever loves as she did:
> Let Mira, your servant, safely cross over,
>   a cow-herding Gokul girl.

Tulsidas. The classic tale of Ram, in the *Ramayana*, was written in Sanskrit, a language not for illiterate people[18]. The story, written in the vernacular dialect of Avadhi, was by Tulsidas. The *Ramacaritmanas (Manas)*, or *The Holy Lake of the Acts of Ram,* is normally chanted by chosen Brahmins and acted out in performance by boys. Its aim was to instruct and to instill a high standard of morality in the readers and in those who were listening. It is acknowledged that Tulsi was a Brahmin and a scholar saint and has been likened to St Jerome. It appears that he may have studied the *Ramayana* and other Sanskrit literature before composing the *Manas.* As a *bhakti* saint, his concerns with language were relevant to all castes, and there may have been tensions between this and being a Brahmin. It was not his intention to destroy the values of the Brahmins, but to demonstrate a different stage of truth. In his poems he employed a sense of ecumenism by attempting to bring religious communities and castes together:

---

18 *In India, where there is a strong oral tradition between the guru and his disciple, to have been illiterate did not mean the same as being ignorant; indeed memorisation was highly esteemed.*

> The fire of my stomach has forced me
> to grasp at the scraps of any caste –
> My caste, high caste, low caste –
> And this in full public display ...

and as well the gods:

> To those who look to hanuman
> The fulfillment of promises is certain,
> like a diamond-cut line in stone,
>
> ... He is favoured by the gods – Parvati, Siva,
> Laksman, Ram and Sita –
> And Tulsi, the gracious gaze from that monkey
> is a mine of good fortune, a mother lode.

The *bhakti* poetry of Tulsidas is grounded in worship, and any spiritual conflicts are resolved by faith in God. As well as his devotion to Ram, Tulsi also dedicated some verses to Krishna and other gods, thus attempting not only to bring together the contemporary religious groups, but also the deities.

In the long history of India there was a culmination in the vernacular languages of the *bhakti* poets through the various cults of the Vedantists, the Sufis, the Alvars and Vaisnaism. Where the two schools of *saguna* and *nirguna* poetry are concerned, from a Western point of view, they may be interpreted as individual paths of devotion and mysticism.

The Bhajan

The *bhajan*, associated with the *Bhakti* movement, was the most popular religious song of North and South India.[19] Both words derive from the Sanskrit stem of *bhaj*, to share in/give/ belong to/serve God in many ways and forms and to seek his blessings. The path of *Bhakti* meant not only sharing with God, but indeed some form of mutual sharing among worshippers was

---

19 *Bhajan in Hindi, quawali in Urdu, abhang in Marathi (Ravikumar, 1996:190)*

expected. *Bhajan* primarily meant that which pleased God and humanity in general and created *ananda* or eternal bliss for the soul. Thus *bhajan* singing proposed to come from the heart, was emotive, and promoted good feelings and pure thoughts. It is said that singing, *bhajans* helped a great deal in encouraging devotion and dedication to God. In general it was said to help wash away all sins, remove darkness or *ajnana*, and lead one to the higher path and ultimately to the feet of God.

The text of the *bhajan* dealt with the attributes of God shown in deeds, as with *avatars* or reincarnations and with his other names:

> Victory to Lord Krishna, also known as Govinda, Mohan, Murari
> … He is the Guru, the Guru of Gurus and the Remover of Sorrows,
> He is the Giver of salvation …[20]

These songs, with many adoring names of God, brought some form of merit, or even some magical power, it was believed, to the *bhakta*. In the religious life of Hindu *Bhakti* it was the practice to make the various names of God objects of constant and loving worship:

> … He is the Creator and the Destroyer of the World
> He is formless, free, eternal and faultless
>
> He is unborn, He is Vishnu and Shiva
> He is the Lord of Gods and the Lord of the three worlds
>
> He is the eternal Song and Composer too
> He is the Note, He is the Speed and the beautiful Rhythm
>
> He is the Father, Mother, Brother, and Wife
> He is the Guru, the Guru of Gurus
> and the Remover of sorrows.
>
> … The poet Adesh says, let us be at his mercy
> *(see Ramlakhan: 40)*

---

20 Ramlakhan, 1994

The plight of the devotee or *bhakta* came under scrutiny:

> ... I am disillusioned with everything ...
> Come and satisfy my thirst.

> No one understands my request
> None understands but you, O Lord.

and:

> Today, let us sing together and give thanks to the Lord
> Whose glories are sung by devotees.

The *bhakta's* hope of salvation was expressed:

> ... when my breath leaves my body,
> may the Lord Krishna be nearby.

Different messages from various saints not only served as an attractive medium of instruction, but also opened up the surest and easiest way for the liberation of the soul, *moksha* (Ravikumar, 1996:192).

> ... Saint Shivanarayana, Sur and Kabir
> By playing the ektara and majeera
> Became immortal, together with Tulsidas and Meera
> By chanting the name of the Lord.

> O my mind, do not place importance on this maya
> Do not be proud of this body
> The poet Adesh says: Chant the name of the Lord
> Through every part of the day and night. *(Ramlakhan: 31)*

Worship in special song services, the *kirtan* or *kalachepans* in Tamil, was skilfully combined with singing. The ancient classics of India like the *Ramayana* and the *Mahabharata* were kept alive through oral tradition by lyrical evangelists who chanted the stanzas and explained their meanings. Large numbers of devotees and pilgrims, sometimes exceeding five hundred, gathered to listen to the exhortations of a famous *sant* or preacher for three or more hours. These *kirtana* were profoundly emotional and the singing of *bhajans* continued night after night, sometimes for weeks. This form of worship may be compared to the *laude* of Francis of Assisi (1182-1226), who through his disciples fostered the Italian *laudesi*, which could be interpreted as the counterpart to the Indian *kirtana* or hymn recitals. Hymns, which were sung in the vernacular language, were accepted by the untutored people of Europe just as the *bhajans* were in India.

The singing of *bhajans* proposed to open the path to the higher reaches of knowledge which removed ignorance and ultimately led to perennial bliss for the soul – *ananda*. Since the language was highly descriptive and the words were of prime importance, simple tunes were composed to please God and obtain *ananda*. In this respect music was seen as tone colouring. Also, as many devotees attending worship in the temples appeared not to be trained in the intricacies of classical forms of music, it may be deduced that the melodies which were developed for *bhajans* were less complicated than the melodies of other sacred Indian musical chants.

In Hindu worship the *bhajan* was a call-and-response form of sung prayer in which the priest sang a simple phrase which was repeated by the devotees. It was also a simple way of learning religious songs, which were composed to underline the Christian theology.

H.A. Popley writes of a boat journey he took in the backwaters of Travancore. The boat had been lent to him by the Metropolitan of the ancient Syrian Christian Church and had twelve native rowers:

> All night long they sang their ancient songs, strange melodies ... sometimes about trees and hills.

and:

> After dinner was over I heard the sound of singing
> coming [from the] temple, and going out, found two
> young men from the village learning the old devotional
> songs from a temple musician. He would sing a line,
> and then they would take it up after him. They were
> simple melodies set to beautiful words of devotion.

The call-and-response style formed the primary character of the *bhajan* composition, and immense care was taken by the leader to include the assembly, whether sung as a simple melody or slightly embellished.

The basic pattern was as follows:
Introduction (optional)

A: Priest or Leader	**A**: Assembly
B: Priest or Leader	**B**: Assembly

Instrumental Interlude (optional)

C: Priest or Leader	**C**: Assembly
D: Priest or Leader	**D**: Assembly

The singing continued along this pattern until all verses were sung, or in some cases, verses were often repeated especially if a new *bhajan* was being learnt.

In Song 1, before formal worship begins, devotees arriving early at a temple in Chaguanas, in Trinidad, encourage each other to be vigorous in their devotion in the following *bhajan* sung on Brothers' Day:

Song 1: *Hindu* bhajan *from Trinidad*

Other forms of the *bhajan* allowed members of the assembly to specialise in one or two songs where there was an exchange of leadership. In some songs the leader introduced the two lines of a couplet and the group sang the second line, thus in effect the second line was sung twice; this apparently continued until everyone knew both lines, or until such time as the leader decided to introduce another couplet. Importantly, the assembly, through repetition, was able to learn the theology which underlined the text as well as the tune.

Another variation was the anticipation of the return to the refrain. The leader sang the last phrase of the refrain after each new verse, and on this signal the group returned to the refrain.

The *nam kirtan bhajan* was a non-strophic text in which the various names and epithets of a deity were chanted. This was believed to endow the devotee with some magical power or bring him some merit.

The *bhajan* sung by many devotees incorporated words of significant importance set to a simple melodic line, and this was maintained in a simple style of repetitive singing. While these *bhajans* were textually inappropriate for the Christian liturgy, the basic call-and-response style of the *bhajan* was adapted by Protestant missionaries in India to reflect a Christian theological understanding of God, Jesus Christ and the Holy Spirit.

CHAPTER THREE

Concepts of Sacred Music in Hinduism

There appear to be two broad, distinct systems of music: that of the Eastern or melodic system, and that of the Western or harmonic system. The former is more ancient, the latter being less than four centuries old. Nevertheless, it would appear that some musical concepts are common to both. For example, Popley is of the opinion that the Indian Gandhara scale, from the Kandahar region, shows an affinity to that of the Greek Doric and Mixolydian scales, which may have been the result of musical fusion.

It was indeed a creative period around 300 BCE - AD 100 in the Greco-Buddhist period. He and other authors compare the division of the Indian scale of twenty-two quarter tones or *scrutis* with that of the Greek scale of twenty-four small intervals. History points to considerable trade and communication between the Greek and Persian Empires, whose musical systems appeared to be similar; on the other hand, communication about music from India is rather obscure, and it is difficult to determine whether there was any interaction of musical systems between other empires in the sixth century BCE. It was in this period that contacts were made between the Greeks and Indians courtesy of the Persians, whose empire was built on that of the Assyrians. In the sixth century the Persian kings extended the borders of their Empire to the Greek Empire in the West and to the Indian in the South East, namely Bactria just North East of the Hindu Kush, and Gandhara to the South East. Greeks and Indians were able to meet and trade and exchanged ideas in the courts of the Persians. There was a distinct oral tradition in the Indian sub-continent, as opposed to that of the Greeks who wrote everything down. The district of Kandahar was a centre of Greco-Indian culture, as shown by sculptures there, as well as those in Taxila (near Rawalpindi), where it is said that Alexander the Great stopped in his conquests from Europe. Greek settler colonies were established. This meant that Greek soldiers were given land and intermarried and soon adopted the local religion. The early Greek-Indians were permanent immigrants whose cultural and economic contribution to the community was welcomed[21]. An early reference to music is made by Panini, who lived around the time that Alexander was in Taxila in 326 BCE. Musical theory c. 400 BCE mentions the three voice registers and the seven notes of the gamut or scale. In the *Ramayana*, the chanting of stories – including musical similes, such as the twanging of the bow and the humming of bees – is mentioned. There are references to musical instruments and *jatis* or *ragas*[22].

The music of the Land of *Bharat* (India, Pakistan and Bangladesh) cannot be divorced from its philosophy and the culture into which it is inextricably woven. A great deal of literature points to the remarkable features of Indian culture – its ability to integrate

---

21 *There was no racism or genocide in the Greek colonies. Unlike the much later European colonizers who controlled local resources through conquest and trade, the Greeks arrived intending to stay permanently, married, had families and adopted the local culture.*

22 *Research is continually finding more evidence of early ancient theories in music.*

many similar facets into a unifying philosophy. Historically, it is seen how the art and music and religion of various races or conquering peoples had assimilated into this vast continent of South Asia. Indeed, with the advent of missionaries from Europe to India in later centuries, here was a tapestry already immersed in several centuries of "foreign" influences into which a Western-style concept of music was soon to be imposed and later absorbed. Sachs is of the opinion that what distinguishes Indian music from the music of Europe is its surprising "stability, tenacity and inertia" (1956: 8-9). It can be conceded that music from the West has developed at an amazing rate from parallel organa to Bach and Byrd, through to Mendelssohn, Howells and John Taverner (born 1944).

Modern scholarship still has problems deciphering records which may show how music developed in the Indian sub-continent; many claims have been made as to several types of systems of Indian music long before the Christian era in Europe. What can be assumed is that over the centuries (as in any developing nation), there evolved art forms of music, both vocal and instrumental, as well as dance disciplines. In view of these developments, rules were established which were to have an influence on the expanding arts, and moreover on an emerging appreciation of the influence of music on the mind.

The belief in Hinduism, as far as the origin of music was concerned, lay in its mythological creation by the god Brahma, and so it was accepted that music was divinely inspired. Music was of God. A song was a *mantra*, "a vocal tool of worship which could lead to an identical consciousness in worshipper and deity" (Holroyd 1972: 67). This belief has continued down through the centuries as Hinduism evolved and developed. This concept of divine sound, although different in a theological context, eventually extended to Christianity, where Gelineau expressed the thought "that music is something divine, and that melody is the daughter of God" (Foley, 1983:22). In Hinduism, music in worship and devotion was emotional. It followed the harmonious flow of nature and was created in association with deities and seasons. In Christianity, a liturgical pattern also evolved according to the birth, death and resurrection of Christ. These patterns in both faiths acted as catalysts for new ideas in ritual and music. The early tribal peoples sang their plainsong to glorify the five godly principles of energy on which humanity was dependent – the sun, air, fire, water and energy or the ether. Music, besides being an art of great beauty and aesthetic pleasure, was also of a joyous and solemn nature. This sacred music was learnt from memory and handed down throughout the centuries. The learning of art forms, be it in secular or sacred forms, demanded a worshipful dedication from the pupil to his master, the *guru*; it demanded intense respect toward age and tradition and knowledge, to long periods of discipline and precise memorisation of technical knowledge. There was no margin for error, so strong was this creative discipline.

During the Gupta period in India (AD 300-500) there was an explosion of architecture, sculpture and painting. These arts combined to create Indian "opera" – the temple with its sacred art and the "stage" with its secular art were the schools of Indian music. This was at a time when, in Europe, Pope Sylvester (AD 330) and St Ambrose (AD 374-397) were working on musical theory. At the same time as a religious revival in South India – the rise of *Bhakti* in the seventh and eighth centuries with its flourishing music school – Gregory the Great in Rome was developing plans for music in religion.

Contrary to Western sources, there were already many musical theoretical sources in India, as indicated by various authors, both Indian and European. Some salient concepts of melody and mode, ornamentation and harmony in Indian music will be dealt with here so as to understand how these in turn had an impact on the acculturation of Western music in India and furthermore on the liturgical music for the Christian *bhajan*.

Figure 3: *Time Chart of Hindu Texts*

Philosophers of Nature (or Rise of Hinduism)	Date (approx)	Three Faiths
Indus Valley Civilisation	c. 2750	
		Abraham of Ur
Vedas	1500 BCE	
	c. 1200	Beginning of Jewish Religion (Worship of Yahweh)
	c. 1250	Exodus from Egypt
	c. 1150	David unites Israel and Judah
	1000 BCE	
	750	Amos – prophet of Israel
Upanishads	700-200	
		Development of Western Thought **(WT)** Homer's Illiad
Bhagavad Gita **(Gita)**	500 BCE	
	497-338	Rise of Greek Classical Culture
	329	Alexander in India
Mahabharata **(M)**; Gita	c. 300 BCE-300 AD	
Ramayana **(Ramay)**; **M**; Gita	200 BCE-200 AD	
	146	Greece under Roman domination
	AD 30	Jesus of Nazareth crucified
St Thomas in India **(Gita; M; Ramay)**	AD 52	
	200	Jewish Mishnah completed; **(WT)**
	c. 200-250	Development of Christian Theology **(CT)**
Gita; M; Ramay Songs of Devotion **(SoD)** *(Bhakti in Hinduism)*	500	
	625	Mohammed begins his mission **(M)**; **CT**
	935	Text of Koran completed; **CT**
Puranas **(P)**; SoD	1000	
	1096	First Crusade; **CT**; **M**
SoD; P	1500	

Music appears to be the oldest of all arts and is acknowledged by many to have absorbed elements from the universe's existence. It was also thought to be coeval with creation. These abstract sounds Pythagoras described as "the music of the spheres". Shakespeare's vision was that the "smallest orb in heaven" which moved made music; the sound of heavenly music could not be heard as long as the "muddy vesture of decay enclosed the soul", as reiterated in *The Merchant of Venice*. This music is precisely what Indian sages referred to as unstruck or inaudible sound, *anahata,* and of which Kabir writes in his poetry:

> There ... the whole sky is filled with sound, and there that music is made *without fingers and without strings* (see Macnicol, 1919: 25).

This unstruck sound is said to be "heard" by those devotees who have achieved a high level of consciousness with the cosmos. The unchangeable musical patterns which are the basis of human existence are said to be heard in the sacred music of the Land of *Bharat.* The power of sound – *ahate*, struck, and *anahata*, unstruck – was said to influence the course of human lives, "leading to total bliss with the divine" (Bake in Wellez, 1957:197).

Historically, more than four thousand years of development, through change, responses to change and consolidation of change, occurred in different parts of India, resulting in a variety of philosophical theologies. It is said that, unlike the Bible, which is a "library" of books, the sacred Hindu scriptures are a library of libraries.

Figure 4: *Major Hindu Scriptures*[23]

The Vedas	1500-1000 BCE
The Upanishads	700-200 BCE
The Mahabharata	300 BCE-AD 300

23 *These dates are approximate. The stories and more information can be read in a vast amount of published literature.*

The Ramayana	200 BCE-AD 200
The Puranas	300-1500 AD
The Bhagavad Gita	500-200 BCE
Songs of Devotion (Bhakti)	700 AD to the present

The *Vedas*, of which there are four, are a collection of philosophy, hymns, stories, rituals and magic, which were composed and collected over centuries. The term *Veda* means insight or knowledge. The *Rig Veda* or *Songs of Praise* contains over one thousand sacrificial hymns, which were devoted to the many gods of nature. A comparison can be made to those of the European mythical gods, for example Dyaus/Pitri was the equivalent to Jupiter or Zeus, and Varuna to Uranus. Included in the other *Vedas* are sacrificial rites in the *Yajur Veda*, melodies for chanting in the *Sama Veda*, and spells and charms in the *Atharva Veda*. The *Vedas* were analysed and explained later by Aryan priests in *The Brahamas*, so as to clarify perplexing rituals contained in the Vedic religion of the time. Contemporary theologians then began to explore the philosophical meaning of life – their existence to humanity and to God. These texts in the *Upanishads* were a collection of philosophical dialogues, in much the same way as the works of Plato and Aristotle. *Upanishad* meant to be sitting near, in that the disciples sat near their masters for tutorials and argued the topic of the day, as in Greek public places. There were around one hundred and eight texts, of which only ten to fifteen were considered; these dealt with the spiritual ideas behind the physical realities of life.

With the advent of Buddhism and Jainism (c. 500 BCE) there was a decline in the sacrificial system, and with the interchange of new religions a new change to Indian philosophy occured. Christianity, five centuries later, played an unwitting part in this fusion of ideas, in that its theological emphasis was on devotion to the Supreme Being. There emerged from this Christian chrysalis the classical Hindu belief of three ways in which devotion to God was to be attained – *Karma Yoga*, which dealt with alterations in the sacrificial scheme, *Jnana Yoga*, in which strands of Buddhism were evident in the search for knowledge, and *Bhakti Yoga*, which focused on devotion to God, borrowing Christian concepts.

The *Ramayana* and the *Mahabharata* were Hindu epics which were orally transmitted down through the centuries and only published in the nineteenth century. They were recited and sung and acted. The *Mahabarata* consisted of almost 100,000 verses and the *Ramayana* of approximately 24,000 verses. Together they are compared in length to Europe's *The Odyssey* and *The Illiad*[24]. The *Puranas*, or *Stories from Ancient Times*, a continuation of the Epics dealt with:

- the creation of the cosmos;
- the recreation of the cosmos after its destruction;
- the genealogies of the gods, sages and kings;
- the ages of the world and their rulers.

The *Puranas* was looked upon as a "handbook" to Hinduism; in it were guides about caste duties, festivals, pilgrim sites and stories of the gods. The *Bhagavad Gita* or *The Song of the Lord*, or *The Divine Song*, not unlike the Psalms in the Old Testament, was a small part of the *Mahabharata* which was added later. It brought together the numerous strands of the beliefs and practices of Hinduism. A latter section of the *Mahabharata* was the *Bhagavad Gita*, in which there were texts of *Bhakti* worship. *Songs of Devotion*, with which this work is concerned, were songs composed and sung in the languages of the people and by the people. They were not in Sanskrit as the great epics were and were not chanted by the priests.

---

24 *Similar subject matter in the Illiad and the Mahabharata describe community ancestral wars. In the Odyssey and the Ramayana, there are tales of foreign wars to rescue abducted royal brides. Evidence in archaeology supports the Illiad; Indian scholars point to the Bharata War c. 3000-1400* BCE *with not enough evidence.*

The sacred scriptures, beginning with the *Rig Veda*, which culminated in the two epics of the *Ramayana* and the *Mahabharata*, followed by the *Gita*, were closely connected with music over a very long period of time. Its author, Valmiki, refers to the humming of the bees as the music of stringed instruments, the thunder of clouds is compared to the beating of drums, and vocal music is like the low moaning of elephants. There are also descriptions of Lakshmana, a deity, listening to music of the vina and other stringed instruments, and accomplished singers as well as Ravana chanting Vedic hymns. There is also mention of *jatis*, the ancient *ragas* and various musical instruments. In the *Mahabharata* the seven notes or *svaras* of the Gandhara[25] Grama is referred to, as well as the theory of consonance.

Figure 5: *Map of Indian Civilisations*

NOT TO SCALE

---

25 *Gandhara was a great distance from the heat of Hindu development; currently there is a lot of research on the music from that area.*

The verses in both works were chanted in musical patterns known as *Samagan* – *sam* meaning melody, and *gan* meaning to sing verses. The vocalisation of sound was an act of worship, which identified the singer with God/Brahma. The metaphysical theory of sound in the *Samgitaratnakara* showed the position of music in the religious system of India. Sound, heard or unheard, became the absolute, in that the music produced had an influence in life which led ultimately to total bliss with the divine. The Sanskrit term, *samgita*, embraced vocal as well as instrumental music, and music for dance. These three art forms formed a triad of which vocal music was the apex.

In looking at these Hindu scriptures it must be acknowledged that there were two main language traditions, one which was Sanskrit in the Ganges Valley, and two, the use of indigenous languages – Tamil in the South and Bengali in the North East. Again an analogy is that of Latin being used in the medieval churches in Europe, followed much later by the use of the national languages of individual countries.

Melody and Modality

Melody, with its system of *scrutis* or microtones as components of tones and semitones, rested on a succession of notes related to each other; when two sounds agreed there was a pleasant sensation. This melodic line was reinforced by the intricacies of *ragas* or scales and *talas* or rhythm patterns. The melodic line in the early sacred chants followed the text in exact detail, the words prescribing the rhythm and flow with no deviations in intonation. Initially, the compass ranged from speech to singing from two notes, which, in the *Sama Veda*, eventually increased to seven notes.

> The musical ear in search of a note does two things. It creeps up or down, one step at a time; and it makes a bold plunge for the nearest consonant note (*samvadi*) from the note

> which has been sounded (*vadi*). The voice has a tendency to
> ascend by leaps and to descend by steps. Music recognises
> the following consonant intervals: the third, the fourth, the
> fifth and the octave. In making a leap to the next consonant
> note, the choice lies between the third and the fourth, as the
> fifth is too far away … The fourth then becomes the upward
> limit of the tetrachord (Popley, 1990: 25-26).

The chants in the *Rigvedic* hymns employed three accents denoting pitch, and these accents indicated a minor or a major third, the middle note being the *udatta*, the lower note the *anudatta* and the upper note the *svarita*. The *Saman* chant was the earliest known Indian tetrachord, which was conceived as beginning from the highest note downwards. The chant pivoted on two notes: the *udatta* and the *anudatta*, and according to Popley, in the course of time the interval of a fourth was established (1921: 27). This led, both he and Sachs believe, to melodies organised in a framework of a falling fourth. Descending steps or jumps, with the prevailing note as the common denominator, formed two tetrachords, one disjunct and the other conjunct. While the conjunct tetrachord shared the prevailing note, resulting in seven notes, the disjunct tetrachord followed a tone apart, resulting in an octave (1963: 11). However, Popley points to a south Indian *raga* which indicates that the *Saman* chant was pentatonic previous to it becoming heptatonic. The songs of early peoples comprised few intervals. When instruments were used as accompaniment, the third and eventually the semitones were added. It was through the use of instruments that the importance of the major third was realised. The vocalist sang the lower notes of the melody, and because of this combination of voice and instrument the scale came into being.

Of crucial importance to the melodic line was the Indian *raga* or scale on which the tune was based. Popley quotes Strangways, who described the *raga* as "an arbitrary series of notes characterised, as far as possible, by proximity to or remoteness from the note which marks the *tessitura* [general level of the melody] by a special order in which they are taken, by frequency or the reverse with which they occur, by grace or the absence of it, and by relation to a tonic usually reinforced by a drone." The term *raga* referred to melodic colour or atmosphere and was a combination of notes which made up melody-like scale patterns; more precisely, the notes which made up the *raga* were taken from a *thatt* or *mela* or mode. The *raga* expressed an emotional feeling and each note evoked a special expression vital to the other notes. The three important notes in a *raga* were the starting note or *graha*, the predominant note the *amsa*, also called the *vadi*, and the ending note or *nyasa*. The *amsa* was described as the soul of the *raga*. The *samvadi*, the second axial note, was a fifth or a fourth from the *vadi*. The other notes were known as *anuvadi*. The *raga* was structurally made up of notes in an ascending order or *aroha*, as well as in a descending order or *avroha*.

Music Example 1: *Raga melodies (ascending and descending)*

A sacred chant or song sung in many ways stayed within the well-defined limits of the *raga,* as to depart from it created an unmusical feeling. The octave or *saptak* consisted of seven notes or *swaras* and may be equated to the Western solfa system (Figure 6). In Indian mythology these names were said to be represented by the sounds of birds or animals[26], and have been described in ancient works by secular music theorists.

---

26 *These are well documented in published literature.*

Figure 6: *The Saptak (Octave)*

Shadai	Sa	C
Rishabha	Ri	D
Gandhar	Ga	E
Maddhyam	Ma	F
Pancham	Pa	G
Dhavat	Dha	A
Nishad	Ni	B

The *raga* expressed a sentiment and each note evoked a special expression which was integral to the other notes. The *ragas* had always been associated with religious practice, and when they were used in secular music, they still retained the deep and spiritual nature because of the Hindu perception that all sound was divinely inspired.

Music treatises suggest that during the Vedic period the Land of *Bharat*, India, possessed the most perfect scale, from which other modes were derived by a shift of the fundamental note. The ancient Indian and Greek systems of music were fundamentally the same in terms of modes, and the Doric scale of the Greek tetrachord was almost identical in form to the oldest form of the Indian tetrachord. Modal Indian music existed by the relationship of the notes to each other, especially the fundamental and prevailing tones, which, like the sound of the bagpipes, was always present in the background or continually sounded.

The dominant factor in Indian music was melody; the melodic line with its *srutis* contained within the confines of the *raga* was essentially and initially vocal, and supplied all melodic interest, but repetition of the same notes was dull. In order to maintain interest over a long period, certain measures were taken besides the limited support of accompanying string and percussion instruments.

Ornamentation

In the melodic line the use of ornaments and embellishment was employed in order to create some variation, namely in the uses of *alamkaras* and *gamaka* or grace notes. The *alamkaras* were ornamental groups of notes, as opposed to single grace *gamaka*. All decorations flowed within the melodic line as if it were part of it and not merely added on. Embellishment in the *gamak* system, with its *alamkaras*, was an organic implement and above all, it was an integral part of the non-harmonic microtonal music of the Land of *Bharat*, and it was elaborate. The combination in the melodic structure of ornamental improvisation within the confines of the *raga*, and the added rhythmical accompaniment on drums, were instrumental in producing a sense of harmony within Indian music[27].

Harmony

It is not to be supposed that Indian music is devoid of harmony. However, the concept of harmony has to be interpreted in a number of ways. As has been said, every note, every *scruti* or microtone was derived from the principle of consonance; that is, every tone in the melody agreed with the fundamental note either directly or through the fourth or fifth. The twenty-two *scrutis* on which the original scale was based were derived by progressions of cycles of fourths and fifths. Notes were interpreted into melody in relation

---

27 *Alain Danielou goes into great depth about the gamaka system (pp 81-85); Popley is very descriptive in his account (pp 83-85). Strangways believed that this Indian instinct could be felt in the music of the Magyars in Europe. The grace notes had a microtonal pitch and the rhythms, if played with less verve, could pass for an Indian accompaniment. He cites an example of a commonly used rhythm which is Indian in style and played on a hand drum or tambour. I have also heard this rhythm employed in improvisation by Paco Peña and Nishat Khan, when the Spanish and Indian percussion players played their respective national drums.*

to the fundamental sound, A note sounded with another note of the same pitch was in unison or concord.[28] Every note left a feeling of its persistence, its harmonics, even after it had been sounded, and this presented a sense of harmony, with the subsequent tone as well as with the previous one. Thus there was a psychological response to harmony in the construction of the melody through the buildup of note to note, to notes, to phrases, and the rendering of continuous musical phrases which were linked. Any break or pause detracted from this sensation of harmony.

Another meaning of harmony in Indian music is the continuous sounding of the drone, which supported the melody and acted as an accompaniment. It acted as a centre of tonal gravity from which the melody and the rhythm returned and departed. The drone was supplied by the *tambura*, whose sounding strings were tuned to the lower fifth, the two key notes and the octave below. In the well-tuned *tambura*, the fifth harmonic as a clear overtone arose as soon as the last string of the lower octave was sounded, thus there was the implication of an harmonic effect always. Importantly, the harmony was always based from the fundamental tone. The richness of the *svara* or musical note was due to the real presence of its overtones; thus every note was harmonious in itself. The vina, sitar, sarangi and other stringed instruments had their own drone strings which were struck regularly during playing, thus adding to the overall timbre effect.

A further interpretation of the concept of harmony is featured in group singing in unison or of the octaves. Bake equates the singing in three octaves to "the low being the breast register, the middle octave the throat register, and the high octave the head register" (see Wellez: 205).

---

28 *When concord or discord is mentioned in relation to harmony in the music of India, it is only in successive use of notes and not in the simultaneous use of notes.*

The three registers or *sthans* were:

(i) the *mandra*, the equivalent to the bass;
(ii) the *madhya*, which corresponds to the tenor or alto;
(iii) the *tar*, or treble register.

The *ati-mandra* was the very low register used by instrumentalists, and occasionally the *ati-tar* or very high register was used. The harmony of combining voices had a powerful appeal in Indian music, and it was in worship in the temple and later in the *kirtan* or hymn gathering where this sense of "togetherness" was keenly felt. In Indian music these concepts of harmony, combined with melody and rhythm, were the basic elements, which resulted in song as the natural expression of man's emotions. Just as dance was the response of the body to the natural instinct of rhythm, so devotional songs became the natural expression of man's religious thought.

CHAPTER FOUR

Missionaries and their Influence on Music in India

Figure 7: *Christianity in India*

NOT TO SCALE

Early Mission History

Early missionaries were in the habit of practising "proper liturgical" music of Gregorian chant and European hymns, the words of which were translated into Indian languages. This was an extension of European church practice, which was at first used by the early pioneers or explorers and later imposed on new converts among the indigenous population. Nineteenth century missionary work in the Indian sub-continent was a continuation of this process, that of mainly introducing Western Christianity with its hymns and music. In the intensive exposure of South Asian society to Western music through church music was the implication that one could not enter the Christian kingdom of God without the Western-styled harmonised hymns.

Historically, one part of the Indian Church is one of the most ancient Christian churches in the world. To their surprise and puzzlement, the first Europeans to visit India in the thirteenth century discovered a flourishing community of Christians known as the Thomas Christians. The tradition of the apostle Thomas coming from Syria by ship in AD 52 and landing in Cranganore is well preserved among the St Thomas Christians of Kerala in South India. An early account is *The Acts of Thomas*, a romance written in the third century[29]. Other documentation is from a Greek writer Cosmas Indicopleuster who had visited India between AD 525-530:

> ... in the island of Taprobane [Ceylon] ... there is a church
> with clergy and a congregation of Christians ... and such
> is also the case in the land called Male where the pepper

---

29 The Acts of St Thomas (a Romance), *was written around the fourth century in the Syriac language, and was later translated into Greek, Latin and Armenian. It dealt with the salvation of souls. It also related how the apostles divided the world among themselves for the purposes of evangelisation of the Christian message. Thomas was unhappy about going to India, but, it is said, the Lord intervened. The Acts then goes on to tell the story of how this happened.*

grows ... The island hath also church of Persian Christians who have settled there, and a presbyter who is appointed from Persia, and all the apparatus of public worship. But the natives and their kings are heathen (Neill, 1970:18).

Indicopleuster, who travelled between 520-525, published his book c. 535, which was the first historical account of the Christian church in South India. Another account pertained to the early Thomas Christians uncovered from a stone slab with a cross with Pahlavi inscription in Mylapore in 1547:

... in the time of the Lord Jesus, Thomas a man of God, was sent by the Son of God (whose disciple he was), to these parts to bring the people of the nation to the knowledge of God, and he built there a temple and wrought great miracles and that finally praying he knelt before that cross and was transfixed with a lance by a Braham; and that that cross remained stained with the blood of the saint for everlasting remembrance. (Brown, 1982:58).

This community of Christians was not of an indigenous nature. They were spice merchants who had settled there and who had links with Babylon. There was also an established Jewish community in Kochi (formerly Cochin), some of whom had been converted to Christianity by Thomas[30]. The Christians who settled along the Malabar Coast were accepted by the local communities and were entrusted with positions at trading posts and public duties such as tax collection on the trade of spices. Their loyalty was to the local *raja* who settled any internal conflict and to whom they turned for support on the later arrival of Portuguese Christians. An example was the appointment by the European Pope of the Jesuit, Father Roz, as Bishop of Ankamali in 1600. The Thomas Christians felt that their church

---

30 *Babylonian/Baghdadi Jewish migration to India is ancient. In part, this migration took place after the fall of the First Temple in Jerusalem over two thousand years ago. In the North, they settled in Bombay and Calcutta, and in the South, in Cochin.*

was downgraded and therefore sought the help of the Raja of Cochin to argue for them. The Raja had given them privileges and concessions, including the collection and sale of pepper and other spices over which the European nations fought.

According to early Western sources, which apparently wished to discredit them as it now appears, this community was connected with the Nestorian heretical sect. Although a heretical form of early Christianity, the term "Nestorian" – often used to indicate the East Syrian and Persian Church – was a geographical rather than a theological one. To the Thomas Christians, this term was a term of derogation and they strongly opposed it, saying that their church was apostolic. There had been political conflict between the Church of Persia and the Eastern Roman Empire, but the Church accepted the decrees at the Council of Nicea[31].

Although these new immigrants accepted many Hindu customs, they were not prepared to accept any religious commitments other than their own. To safeguard their own religion, two measures were enforced: one, their bishops had to come from their original homeland; and two, the language of the liturgy was to be conducted in Syriac – hence they were referred to as "Syrian" Christians.

Archaeological finds also point to the foreign traders marrying local inhabitants. In 1547, near Madras, the Portuguese dug up an ancient stone cross with an inscription in an unknown language. This was translated in 1928 as "My Lord Christ, have mercy on Afras, son of Chaharbukt the Syrian, who cut this" (Neill, 1970:31). In the *Anglo-Saxon Chronicles*, 883, there was an entry which read that Sighelm, Bishop of Shereburn, was sent to the

---

31 *Constantine founded Constantinople in AD 330 and became its ruler in 324. There was controversy among various groups concerning the divinity of Christ. To settle this once and for all, and in attempting to unite the various fractions, he called the first eccumenical conference of the Church at Nicea in 325. The statement "of one essence" to describe Christ's relationship to the Father became one of the great creeds in Christianity.*

tomb of St Thomas in India by Alfred the Great in fulfillment of a vow (Paul, 1952:13). Popley wrote touchingly of an experience which haunted him:

> I can remember [a] night on the back-waters of Travancore in the extreme south-west of India. I was in a boat ... been lent by the Metropolitan of the ancient Syrian Christian Church ... All night long they sang their ancient songs, strange melodies ... sometimes about trees and hills and forests, and sometimes about the Virgin Mary, for they were Catholics ...

and:

> all day long the songs go on: primitive folk tunes, and in some Christian villages the Psalms as set to these old tunes by the early Christian missionaries[32].

In 1999 a British television crew, filming for a documentary programme about Kerala, came across a wall painting of what was possibly a portrait of the Apostle Thomas hidden behind the altar of an ancient church.

When the Portuguese traders discovered this ancient community of Christians, it may be assumed that both churches were equally surprised and delighted to find out about the existence of each other and may have even considered each other as "allies". Political conflicts in the early centuries of the early Christian churches between the Roman and Persian Empires led some churches to assert their autonomy on the basis of apostolic tradition; the scene was now set for an eruption concerning the interpretations of theological concepts. Here was a liturgy of the Thomas Christians, which was later to evolve with a mixture of cultures, pre-Latin Christianity in an Indian environment and oriental in worship – or as Rev. A.T. Mammen said, "The Mar

---

32 *In the Kerala State and its Backwaters, many churches and roadside chapels have been built. These places of worship remain open, and are used frequently, as the author observed.*

Thoma Syrian Church [of India] is Eastern in worship, Episcopal in tradition, ecumenical in vision and Catholic in mission"[33].

The St Thomas Christians had links with Mesopotamia and had received their bishops from there. They had not heard of the Pope and took umbrage at being accused of Nestorian heresy. They had received, they maintained, the true faith from their founder, the Apostle Thomas, and although they had assimilated Hindu secular customs, they nevertheless had scrupulously avoided any form of idolatry. To them it was anathema and shocking, and a great disappointment, to find that the Romans exhibited statues and images in church. On the other hand, the Romans could not understand that here were Christians who did not acknowledge the Roman Father. Throughout the sixteenth century the relationship between these two sects of Christians was greatly strained. A vexed question was that pertaining to the Syrian Rite of the liturgy, which was considered indigenous and inculturate by the St Thomas Christians, who opposed the meddling of the Portuguese missionaries and colonists. In 1599 the Archbishop of Goa called together a synod of the Malankara Church at Diamper and brought the church under the control of the Roman Pope. Unable to bear the authoritarian attitude and tactless policies of the Roman Church, the Thomas Christians gathered round the Leaning Cross (Coonen Kurisu) at Mattancherry and pledged to sever the Roman connection. As a result, thirty-two parishes maintained their independence. Needless to say, after the rebellion of the Coonen Cross, Roman Catholics and Syrians lived uneasily beside each other. The independent Syrians maintained some contact with Mesopotamia, although they had no bishops over a long period of time.

---

33 *Personal correspondence, April 1998. Rev. A.T. Mannen was pastor at the Mar Thoma Church in London and has written a short history of the church for his congregation.*

Under the British, communication through the Church Missionary Society (CMS) began. Missionaries were under strict instructions not to convert the Syrians to Anglicanism, but to help in education and training for the ministry of their own people who had accompanied them for administrative purposes. The service in Syriac was unintelligible to the people, and very little of the Bible was in the local language of Malayalam. This was later rectified and younger members who read the Bible became critical of the older traditions. In 1835 a break occurred between the missionaries and the Metropolitan Dionysius IV. Education was maintained and Syrian students attended the CMS College in Kottayam. Inevitably, a schism between the Syrians grew as many valued and turned to the simple Anglican service. This was accepted reluctantly, and future leaders were to emerge from 1879-1947 in the Anglican diocese of Travancore and Cochin, the first Indian bishop being C. K. Jacob. A small percentage of Syrians joined the Church of England, while the majority was faithful to the old church.

Beneath the surface new rumblings were beginning to sound. Like any renaissance, new concepts were being developed by the Thomas Christians. Abraham Malpan, the Syriac teacher at Kottayam, acknowledged the need for reform in the light of new biblical knowledge being disseminated by missionaries and was against any schism[34]. In the aftermath of the climax in 1879, an independent Eastern Church emerged. The Roman Catholic or Malankara sections of the church held together, combining many of the ancient traditions of the church with simple biblical teaching and an evangelical ethos. More than two generations were to pass before the strife was healed, helped by the Anglo-Catholic wing of the Anglican

---

34 *Abraham Malpan was a teacher at the Kottayam Seminary and was invited to help in the Anglican Church in Kerala, but decided to stay in the Mother Church.*

Church and the Oxford Mission to Calcutta[35].

While the St Thomas Christian Church and the European Church were arguing with each other and going through a period of upheaval – establishing and consolidating their differences and agreeing to differ – in the North another faith had made great conquests and had established permanent communities. History shows that it was the great Mogul Empire with whom the Europeans had to deal. Akbar (1556-1605), the greatest of all the Mogul rulers in India, put into place many laws, showed tolerance to the many faiths and allowed free debate to take place[36]. It is said that he was the first instigator of inter-faith dialogue. At his court were Taoist and Confucian scholars from China, Hiyayana monks from Sri Lanka, Muslims from Kabul and further afield, among many visitors and delegations from foreign countries; and from the sub-continent Buddhists, Jains, Hindus, Muslims and Sikhs were present. This great Mogul emperor of India studied the doctrines of other religions, including Christianity, which flourished without hindrance, as he was unhappy with the dogma of orthodox Islam. This exploration led to the formation of his

35 There were many divisions within the Thomas Christian Church after the
    arrival of missionaries from Europe. Some of the St Thomas Christian
    Groups are (1) Anglican: Mar Thoma Church; (2) Evangelical Protestant:
    St Thomas Evangelical Church; (3) Oriental Orthodox Communion:
    Indian Orthodox Church or the Malankara Orthodox Syrian Church;
    Malabar Independent Syrian Church; (4). Catholic: Syro-Malabar
    Catholic, Syro-Malakara Catholic Churches.

36 The Mogul Emperors who ruled India were Baber (1526-30), Humayun
    (1530-56), Akbar (1556-1605), Jahangir (1605-27), Shah Jehan (1628-58)
    and Aurangzeb (1658-1707). After the death of the last emperor, a rapid
    decline followed. In his lifetime Akbar undertook innovative measures for
    his new kingdom – he divided his government into legislatures, introduced
    a land revenue system, organised the country into cities and provinces
    with local officials, currency was standardised, peasants were reimbursed
    for the spoiling of their land by the conquering military. Among his many
    achievements he invented a new system of weights and measures, instituted
    a mail system, made administrative records obligatory, outlawed child
    marriages and infanticide, and set up a civil service.

own religion, the *Din-i Ilahi*, which did not last after his death. Its rules were simple and were drawn from strands of other faiths – prayers were to be said three times a day, there was no eating of meat, the principles of reincarnation and *karma* were accepted, debates were to be tempered with gentleness, and kindness to all living creatures was to be shown. At Fatephur Sikri he designed and built the *Ibadat Khana*, "the House of Worship", to which theologians were invited from far and wide to discuss religious issues.[37] Fascinated by Christianity, he invited representatives from Goa. The Italian Rudolfo Aquqviva and the Spanish Antonio Monserrate were greeted with great kindness, and from them Akbar learnt about this faith. He was given a copy of the Plantin Bible, had a large crucifix over his bed and wore a miniature cross around his neck. Needless to say, this mission was not successful, as the Muslims would not have tolerated their Emperor's conversion; also Akbar was unwilling to jeopardize his alliances with the Hindus by adopting a creed opposed to the fundamental dogmas of his allies.

Fatephur Sikri (HJN)

---

37 *This vast estate had to be abandoned later when the water dried up; it still stands in all its majesty as a reminder of Akbar's exploits.*

Christianity also played a part in the court of his son, Jahangir, "the World Seizer" (1606-1627). Images of the Virgin Mary were present, and it is said that he almost converted to Christianity – not because of belief, but because it was suitable for his needs. Jahangir also attended mass in the Catholic Church built by Akbar the Great.

In the South, meanwhile, the Portuguese aimed to reproduce in India life as it had been in Portugal, and it was at Goa that some major Roman Catholic Orders established convents. Initially, there was no strong inclination to convert the indigenous people, but idolatory was unacceptable and could not be tolerated on the territory of a Christian king. Trade was the crucial objective, followed by ministry to their own people. This was to change with the arrival of Francis Xavier in Goa in 1542.

Francis Xavier (1506-1552) was a companion of Ignatius Loyola and belonged to the Society of Jesus. Xavier's first task was to minister to the church in Goa. He then turned his attention to the Coromandel Coast where the fisher people, the Paravas (the Bharathas), had requested protection from sea and land pirates. This was done only after they were baptised. Xavier was responsible for introducing a form of catechetical instruction involving a great deal of repetition which included the Lord's Prayer, the Apostles' Creed and the Ten Commandments.

> On Sunday I assemble all the people, men and women, young and old, … I give out the first commandment which they repeat, and then we say together, Jesus Christ, Son of God, grant us grace to love thee above all things. When we have asked for this grace, we recite the Paternoster of Jesus Christ, obtain for us grace from thy Son to enable us to keep the first commandment … and so on through all the other commandments (Neill : 32).

Xavier was buried in Goa.

Roberto de Nobili, an Italian Jesuit, arrived in Madura in 1606. He found that the Portuguese custom of Europeanising converted Christians had a negative effect on potential converts from Hinduism. He totally immersed himself in the food, the dress and the manners of a Brahmin and learnt Tamil, Telegu and other Indian languages, as well as classical Sanskrit. De Nobili came to a Westernised un-Indian church. He mastered the *Vedas* and the *Vedanta* so as to use Indian philosophy and language as a vehicle for conveying Christian theological thinking. It could be said of de Nobili that his action was the first example of a process of inculturation by a European; he also allowed the wearing of the sacred thread (the sign of twice-born castes), which was put on with Christian prayers. There was fierce opposition to his practice of inculturation, but after much dissension, Rome found in his favour in 1623. This was to pave the way for the reforms of Vatican II in the twentieth century.

Other Jesuit missionaries followed de Nobili, including Beschi, who adopted the manner of a Hindu guru and mastered the Tamil language. He produced the *Tembavani* or *Unfading Garland,* which was a literary work as long as the *Odyssey,* in which he related the gospel story. In South India, where the Jesuits carried out their missionary work, there also followed the orders of the Augustinians, the Franciscans and the Dominicans.

Thomas Stevens, the English Jesuit, arrived in Western India in 1579. Stevens, realising the hold that the vernacular *Puranas* had on the minds of the people, composed a Christian *Purana*, a long poem narrating the stories of the Old and New Testaments in colloquial Marathi. He mastered the Konkani language and left an immense *purana*, an historical composition, based on the Old Testament and the gospels in metrical form which could easily be read by the ordinary people.

Not wanting to be left out of the competition for new discoveries of land and trade, other European countries followed. In 1673 the French founded a colony at Pondicherry. Earlier the Dutch had captured Cochin (1633). The question of "accommodation" – the will to disrupt as little as possible the life and customs of the converts – engineered by the Jesuits was rejected totally. Christianity in India was the reflection of Christianity in Rome. Sadly, some Indian Christians who trained as catechists were not admitted to the priesthood. By 1750 it was recognised that the Christian churches in India "lacked zeal, courage and hope of further great achievement." (Neill, 1970:47)

The emerging and passing Protestant European nations influenced the church in India. The sea power nations of France, Britain and Holland were followed by Germany and Norway. After the formation of the British East India Company in 1600, the Dutch and Danish nations were determined to forge ahead in trade and ignored the previous powers of Spain and Portugal. The Dutch and the English were in agreement in their dislike for the Roman Catholics, and eventually the Dutch left to trade in Indonesia, leaving the British to develop the Indian market. The first British settlement was at Surat on the West coast, and to this was added Fort St George, Madras, Fort St David, Cuddalore and the mud flats of Calcutta and the island of Bombay.

The English Company trading in India provided chaplains to all the main stations to ensure that prayers were said twice daily in workplaces, as well as on Sunday. Missionary zeal from Europe, Scotland and America was such that schools and colleges were established and printing presses were set up in order to disseminate the Christian message. Bibles and religious literature were printed in many Indian languages, and South Asians were trained for the ministry. Without realising it, the ruling power of Great Britain was laying the foundations for future East Indian missionary work to an Indian work force in the British island colonies of Mauritius, Fiji and the Caribbean.

Figure 8: *Map of British Interests*

NOT TO SCALE

Music

The earliest Christian missionaries to India, and those who followed later with their attendants, brought with them forms of ritual and music which were practised in their countries of origin. Undoubtedly, they would have attempted to impose their forms of worship and music on local churches in South India. Syncretic styles of monody may have resulted in combined styles of chants in Hinduism with those of early European sacred music as missionaries attempted to make their converts feel "at home". Here were styles – a European monodic chant, an

Indian style of monody and a harmonic European style – which may have impacted on each other as a result of an approximate degree of compatibility. Hypothetically, if the mission colonies devoted a relatively constant energy to a new form of Christian Indian worship music, most of this energy might have been directed to a new musical style unknowingly. Adaptation might have involved a reduction of European Christian monodic repertoire, or in the number of musicians in both traditions. Unfortunately, any such musical styles used in the early mission programme are unknown. What can be surmised is that any impact of both monodic styles supported by Western music harmonisation paved the way for later missionaries and their influences on ritual and music in Christian worship.

In secular India the earliest chroniclers of Indian music were the British colonial administrators, as well as European travellers. India, unlike other ancient cultures of Greece, Rome and Egypt, was a living culture which could be analysed. British interest in Indian music would have been negligible except for several significant works. Among the many studies was a treatise – *On the Musical Modes of the Hindoos* (1792) – by Sir William Jones, who was a leading oriental scholar in Greek, Latin, Hebrew, Arabic, Persian, Chinese and Sanskrit. His treatise was based on original Indian sources and opened the way for the study of the highly sophisticated music of India by Western scholars. Captain N. Augustus Williard, who was attached to a princely state in Uttar Pradesh in 1834, wrote *A Treatise on the Music of Hindustan* (1834), commenting on the gap over the centuries between Indian musical theory and its practice. His work included factual and accurate descriptions of forms and glossary terms. Fox Strangways in 1914 wrote *Music of Hindostan* in which his comments on Indian music and his analogies with Western music are revealing. Two other notable persons who contributed to scholarly works were Sir

W. Ousley and Captain Charles Russell Day of the Oxfordshire Light Infantry, who wrote *The Music and Musical Instruments of Southern India and the Decan* (1891). His description of the Karnatak system of music was widely read.

There was also an important attempt at collaboration between British and Indian musicologists, such as K.B. Deval and Ernest Clements, who collaborated on the subject of scales. Some of the earliest sources for popular devotional tunes and texts are to be found in Christian hymnals compiled by missionaries – Parsons 1861, Ullmann 1878, and Bate 1886[38]. Another collaboration was between V. N. Bhatkhande and H.A. Popley. Bhatkhande (1860-1936) trained in vocal and instrumental music, spoke several Indian languages as well as English, studied law and carried out meticulous research on ancient theories of music. Reviews of important Sanskrit sources led him to introduce new concepts in order to explain the musical practice of his day, acknowledging the influence of many traditions on Indian music. He was also complimentary about the considerable influence of music from the Islamic culture. He researched the many music schools throughout India. The *gurus* and *ustads* of the *gharanas* were at first reluctant to accommodate him, but eventually yielded to his insistence because of his vast knowledge and enthusiasm. As a result he was able to carry out and classify the *thatt* system of *ragas*, reducing them to ten[39]. In order that these *thatts* would be recognised, they were named after popular *ragas* with the note C as Sa:

---

38 *There is considerable research in music taking part in India, which has been described in numerous papers.*

39 *N.A. Jairazbhoy in 1971 worked out scientifically that there could be 32 thatts.*

Thatt	Notes
Bilaval	Sa Re Ga Ma Pa Dha Ni
Kayal	Sa Re Ga Ma♯ Pa Dha Ni
Khamaj	Sa Re Ga Ma Pa Dha Ni♯
Bhairav	Sa RE♭ Ga Ma Pa Dh A♭ Ni
Purvi	Sa RE♭ Ga Ma♯ Pa Dh A♭ Ni
Marva	Sa RE♭ Ga Ma♯ Pa Dha Ni
Kafi	Sa Re Ga♭ Ma PA Dha NI♭
Asavari	Sa Re Ga♭ Ma Pa DhA♭ NI♭
Bhairavi	Sa RE♭ GA♭ Ma Pa DHA♭ NI♭
Todi	Sa RE♭ GA♭ MA♯ Pa DHA♭ Ni

(Massey, 1993:102).

Bhatkhande also realised that the practice performance of Indian music was leaning towards the twelve semitones of the Western scale with some variations; he therefore worked out a relationship between both.

Indigenous musicians were trained in order to assist the colonisers and missionaries in adapting Indian tunes to music for Western consumption. The colonisers were amateurs and not skilled in musical analysis. Their interest in India's classical and folk music was regarded as a source of information about the people of the land they governed – the languages, the beliefs and the customs. Although British politics was to shape Western disciplines in India from law to archaeology, there was a pragmatic need to understand the peoples of India in order to operate effectively the British missions in trade, government, social reform and later on in missionary work. The need to understand the music was, in part, an indicative factor of the land they governed. Ironically, much of this adapted music was preserved in Western notation and in English, which rendered it inaccessible to most people in India; happily there is a process of addressing this issue currently.

Where missionaries were concerned, they would have followed the same method used by their fellow men in adapting music for Christian worship, as well as introducing hymns from the West. In the secular communities, Indian musicians had to adapt European methods in order to process the notating of Indian melodies. Woodfield points to Margaret Fowke's method, which was to get Indian musicians to tune their instruments to her harpsichord so that she could play along with them:

> I have often made the musicians tune their instruments to the harpsichord that I might join their little band. They always seemed delighted with the accompaniment of the harpsichord and sang with uncommon animation ...[40]

The use of a keyboard in this context, as Strangways had earlier intimated, was to destroy the intonation of the melodic system inherent in Indian music. As far as European musicians were concerned, they were helping to preserve the folk tunes of a land they governed and had little inkling that they were destroying the original. There was the added problem of the keyboard not being in tune, due to the dismal tuning skills of Europeans in India. This may have resulted in the portable harmonium being employed in the religious sector as missionaries and their assistants did much peripatetic work in preaching the gospel.

The hand pump harmonium with fixed, diatonic pitch was patented by the French instrument maker, Alexandre François Debain in 1842, and was widely disseminated in India by British missionaries in the nineteenth century. It was a small portable instrument set in a box and was played while sitting on the floor. This instrument was to exert a strong influence on the concepts of pitch and melody. Used to accompany singers, the tuning varied with each instrument.

There was a diverse number of individuals involved in the

---

40 British Journal of Ethnomusicology, *1994, Volume 3: 76.*

processing of notation – the Indian performer, the Indian linguist, the European linguist, the European "professional"/amateur musician.

Attempts to record an adaptation of Indian sacred tunes followed a common format which was also prevalent in secular society. The process of adapting an Indian melody, in a style with which Europeans could associate, was by writing down the melody and adding a bass line and chords, all of which was an alien concept to Indian music[41]. Also, traditional harmonic arrangements for four voices – soprano, alto tenor and bass – were made.

In adapting these melodies, the natural link between melody and harmony was the use of chord I and chord V, which was associated with the fundamental tone and its prevailing tone of the Indian *raga*. A typical example was the hymn *Yisu ne Kaha*, "Jesus the Lord said, I am the Bread", a version of which is to be found in hymnbooks. Other adaptations of tunes and words can be seen in many worship songbooks in India, Great Britain, the Caribbean and countries of the diaspora, where tunes are termed "anonymous" or "adapted from Urdu". It is very likely that these transcriptions were used by missionaries who wished to communicate the Christian message, through song, to Christian South Asians and to new converts. However, traditional singing, dancing and drumming, which were integral forces within Indian music, were expressly forbidden by missionaries as they were deemed "pagan".

Some elements of Indian music, such as melodic lines, modes, ornamentation and the use of drones which were identified as being similar to European music, were arbitrarily transcribed

---

41 *Woodfield (1994, 73-77) has made a study of many melodies which appear in the Fitzwilliam Manuscript (MS 380), Cambridge. Many of these airs were collected by Sophia Plowden in India, and used by William Crotch (1808-15) in his compositions.*

into Western thinking. The emphasis on improvisation and its virtuosity inherent in Indian music was ignored, as it was deemed unsuitable for congregational participation. The rhythmic systems appeared to defeat the missionaries and other transcribers, so that many melodies were given European time signatures and classed as anonymous.

This amateur procedure of early transcripts, which were solely for European taste, was aptly described by Farrell:

> With the very first act of transcription, Europeans started to change the music they heard to fit the written page, and the few remaining hints of the original Indian melodies occur only in general melodic contour and occasionally in the intervals used ... such was the power of staff notation to discipline a music that was generally viewed as unruly and formless, albeit charming by Europeans.[42]

The twentieth century saw a process of indigenisation of Christian ritual and music which was sanctioned by both Roman Catholic and Protestant churches in India. The introduction of Western elements was governed by two factors – compatibility and the accompanying possibility of producing syncretic results for worship. In order to carry out the work for which they were trained, and succeed in its development, the missionaries had to find some vehicle to reach their potential flocks. The simple style of the *bhajan* from the *Bhakti* movement appeared to fulfill this requirement. Its repetitive call-and-response form was to lend itself to the teaching of Christian theology in text and in music.

In a culture which had graciously absorbed new styles, and continued to do so, and made it their own, the *bhajan* would prove to be remarkably successful in Christian worship throughout India and in the countries of its diaspora.

---

42 *Farrell, 1997:19. I also had an opportunity to discuss this and other matters relating to Indian music with Gerry before his untimely death.*

CHAPTER FIVE

Christian *Bhakti* as Lyric

A strong theistic tradition of *bhakti* was already in existence throughout India during the growth of the Christian Church in the sub-continent. Rudolf Otto has described the tradition of *bhakti* religion as "faith in salvation through an eternal God and through a saving fellowship with Him". And so it was felt, especially by missionaries, that this tradition could be employed in leading many towards the Light of Christ.

The features of *Bhakti* thought maintained by the system of Ramanuja, *vishishtadvaita* or "modified monism" were attractive to Indian Christians. Ramanuja (traditionally 1017-1137) was a devotee of Vishnu and was one of the leaders of the *Alvars*. In this patriarchal society, he advocated that the holy scriptures should be available to all people, including women, and was responsible for reforming and consolidating theological concepts of *Bhaktism*. Like Sankara before him, he also believed that God was the Supreme One. Sankara (788-820) was born to a Brahmin couple. His commentaries on the Vedas and Upanishads attracted many disciples. His philosophy was known as *advaita* or absolute monism based on the Upanishads. Madhava (c. 1200), whose philosophy was *dvaita* or dualism, saw God, the world and the soul as distinct and salvation as the grace of God to the devotee. God, in Sankara's terms, was the soul in the world, but even with the knowledge, warmth, love and personal devotion of the worshipper, what was needed was God's grace. This was a familiar concept to the Indian Christian and a path that could be accessed.

The beginnings of Christian *Bhakti* began to manifest itself in the early years of the nineteenth century. Christian poets in Tamil Nadu, who were converted to Christianity and who were deeply steeped in the *Bhakti* tradition of Hinduism, began to write Christian lyrics, which presented an offering of loving devotion or *bhakti* to Christ. The works of two such poets, Krishna Pillai (1827-1900) and Narayan Vaman Tilak (1862-1919), will be considered in this context.

The theology of *Krishna Pillai* was very much that of the evangelical missionaries with whom he came into contact. Born into a high caste non-Brahmin family, he was also a teacher at the Christian Mission Society College at Tiruelveli. Appasamy points to the fact that Pillai recognised that if Christianity was to be successful in India, it had to become Indian in its worship, in its theology and in its church literature and church government[43]. Having read Bunyan's *Pilgrim's Progress*, Pillai was inspired to write a Tamil Christian classic which interpreted his personal experience of the Christian faith. In the book *Rakshanya Yatrikam*, "The Journey of Salvation", he wrote many devotional lyrics in

---

43 *Bishop Aiyadurai Jesudasen Appasamy (born 1891) was an Indian theologian who identified himself with the Bhakti tradition; he looked to the personalist tradition of Bhakti and to its philosophical exposition found in Ramanuja. His personal contact with writers such as Von Hugel, Otto and Echart deeply interested him and shows some influence in his works of his own Tamil devotional poets.*

the style of Tamil Hindu lyrics. The *Rakshanya Yatrikam* was published in 1894 and consisted of four thousand stanzas, among which were many devotional lyrics also in the style of Tamil Hindu lyrics. Appasamy himself remembered attending a *kalachepan* or *kirtan*, which went on for weeks, on the occasion of Pillai's epic being narrated, at which more than five hundred people were present. The cast who related the epic were accompanied by three men who played violins and a small drum. In Pillai's poetry the central figure was Christ:

> he [Pillai] longed for the power to express to his people
> the beauty and dearness of Christ Jesus his Redeemer, by
> whose stripes he was healed[44].

Krishna Pillai's poetry conveys a very strong sense of the power of sin and of Christ, who accepted those sins by dying on the Cross. With his background of Hindu literature in Tamil and Sanskrit, both Boyd and Appasamy agree that Pillai's own rich poetic imagination became the crucible in which the Christian faith was given an attractive Indian form while remaining essentially the same.

One of his poems speaks of God as King Saccidananda. As a name for God, Saccidananda was popular in religious circles in India. It signified the mystery of the divine presence in the soul of man; God was its guest. The term Saccidananda comprised three Sanskrit words, *Sat* or existence, *Chit* or knowledge and *Ananda* or joy. Further explanation in Hinduism describes *Sat* as that which does not change, therefore God remains the same although many things around him change. God is *Chit*, that is, he is the Mind behind the universe where there should be no chaos, but order and unity among all living things. God is *Ananda*; what he has created is a source of great joy to him. In reference to the Bible these were not the

---

44 H.A. Krishna Pillai *by Amy Carmichael, pages 21-22. In her biography of Pillai, Carmichael writes of his deep Christian devotion, and was at his bedside when he died.*

only attributes of God. Other qualities, from a Christian perspective noted in Pillai's poetry, talk of His holiness and love, which balance the other qualities of His existence, knowledge and joy[45].

In another stanza the Christian Trinity replaces the *trimurti* of Brahma, Vishnu and Siva. Motherhood, as in *Bhakti* poetry, is also seen as a characteristic of God:

> He who matched the three-fold powers
> Of creation, preservation and destruction,
> With the Trinity of Father, Son and Holy Spirit;
> The God in Whom the Three are One,
> And who is One in Three;
> Holy one in body, speech and mind;
> In form the peerless Mother of all good deeds
> And all worthy to be praised-
> Himself the precious Medicine for sin
> 'Tis He I see upon the Cross.[46]

Pillai's descriptive poetry of the living Ganges is likened to Christ's coming into the world:

> At compassion's cool caress.
> It took on visible form, men's souls to save;
> Coming down from high Heaven, strange to behold!
> Its course ran straight in the path ordained,
> And never overflow the bounds set at yore.
> Love ripening, it poured life into the wide world
> And saved it from death and decay!
> This is the flow of the Holy Lord's
> compassion – the Living Ganga!

---

45 *At the International Eucharistic Congress of the Roman Catholic Church in Bombay (1964), Cardinal Gracias, Archbishop of Bombay, decided to present to the delegates a form of Christian worship with a distinctive Indian setting. Father Georg Proksch, a German musician and scholar, trained a choir of one thousand voices and three hundred dancers to perform the story with Indian music and dance. A hymn book was published for the Congress in which there was a hymn addressed to Saccidananda.*

46 *The following quotes are by Appasamy (1966:51), except where Boyd is indicated.*

Christ is compared to the Ganges, which, as the heavenly Ganga, takes away sin:

> It washed clear away the slimy sin – Man's heritage!
> It became also food and drink for him – pure and satisfying!
> Thus nourished the Life of Wisdom ever grew
> Yielding the fruit of Salvation true!
> Such was the blood of our Savior – Immanuel –
> Shed for all – the living Ganga.

The work of salvation is described in terms of a swimmer rescuing a drowning man, which is a picture often used in Indian Christian lyrics.

> In the river of death, into which it rained its water,
> the majestic Saviour swam all alone,
> with countless souls underneath His arm (Boyd, 1969: 116)

In one canto, Pillai described and meditated on the events of Holy Week – the pain and suffering which Christ underwent, the malice of his enemies, the love of his disciples. According to Appasamy, "he developed his thoughts with minute care and genuine insight in five hundred stanzas". In the resurrection of Christ, Pillai used metaphors of nature to describe the wonder that men and angels experienced on that eventful morning:

> The mountain spring murmured in its spray;
> And the birds twittered in the wood;
> From these sounds mingling rose sweet music …
> … The wood was gay
> With blooms of varied hue …

Pillai's songs adoring the names of God in a "thousand" ways were written not to win merit, but in remembrance of what Jesus did for mankind:

… Sweet ambrosia to the sinner is
The Name of the Lord Jesus …

It is the Revelation clear!
It is the meaning entire of Holy Writ!
It is the nurturer of Grace and Love …

It is life everlasting;
… It is wisdom pure; it is the abode of Truth …

Several images used in Christian *Bhakti* literature describe Christ. He, Christ, is the river of life from heaven and the mountain of salvation, the ocean of bliss, the cloud that showers the rain of grace, life-saving medicine, gem of gems. Poets and singers who were steeped in the *Bhakti* tradition endeavoured to forge a sense of Indian Christianity by using their lyric ability and vocabulary, with which they were imbued from Hinduism, and indeed Pillai's works demonstrate that he was outstanding in this context because of his faith.

Narayan Vaman Tilak, who was a Christian poet, was a leader in the movement of the romantic revival in Marathi literature at the end of the nineteenth century. His Christian poems included many lyrics which were, and still are, used in congregational worship, as well as for evangelisation. Tilak's ambition was to write a narrative epic on the life of Christ, but he was only to complete part of the *Christayan*. There was an intensity of devotion in his poetry, which was expressed in the following:

Tenderest Mother-Guru mine,
Saviour, where is love like Thine?

A cool and never fading shade
To souls by sin's fierce heat dismayed.

Right swiftly at my earliest cry
He came to save me from the sky:

He made him friends by those who mourn
With hearts by meek contrition torn:

For me, a sinner yea, for me
He hastened to the bitter Tree:

And still within me living, too,
He fills my being through and through,

My heart is all one melody –
"Hail to Christ! all hail to Thee!" (Boyd, 1969).

The Hindu *bhakti* poet Tukaram[47] had been resigned to fate:

Here tower the hills of passion and lust;
Far off the Infinite.
No road I find, and all impassible
Fronts me the hostile height (Macnicol, 1919:130).

For Tilak this was not so:

As the moon and its rays are one – so, that I be one with Thee,
That is my cry to Thee, O God, that is this beggar's plea (Ibid).

In the same genre as in the poems of the Hindu poets, Namdev and Tukaram, Tilak's poems express the longing of the soul of the *bhakta* for union with God:

The more I win Thee, Lord, the more for Thee I pine;
Ah, such a heart is mine (Boyd, 1969:116).

Tilak's innocent wonder is shown in his hymns on the atonement; there are simple expressions of love and of honest amazement at God's suffering and His grace:

Hast thou ever seen the Lord, Christ the Crucified?
Hast thou seen those wounded hands?
Hast thou seen His side? (Ibid).

---

47 *Tukaram was a Maratha bhakta and was successful in his attempts in drawing together a common religious enthusiasm in a united community, which resisted the power of the Mogul Empire. His abangs (bhajans) are said to have form and authority of proverbs.*

In some of Tilak's poems there is a deep longing for India to accept Christ, and for the Church to become truly Indian:

> When shall these longings be sufficed
> That stir my spirit night and day?
> When shall I see my country lay
> Her homage at the feet of Christ? (Ibid).

The following lines describe the nature of union with Christ who represents the deepest level of salvation for the Christian *bhakta*:

> As the moon and its beams are one,
> So, that I be one with Thee,
> This is my prayer to Thee, my Lord,
> This is my beggar's plea.
>
> I would snare Thee and hold Thee ever
> In loving, wifely ways;
> I give Thee a daughter's welcome,
> I give Thee a sister's praise.
>
> Take Thou this body, O my Christ,
> Dwell as its soul within,
> To be an instant separate I count a deadly sin (Macnicol, 1919:130).

In the words of Macnicol, his friend and translator, Tilak "brought together and fused the Christian message and the great Hindu tradition of *Bhakti*" ... Tilak brought to the Maratha Church a renaissance of poetry, literature and religion "where even the outcaste Christians were able to sing of their appropriation of Christ as well as their Indian heritage". He made an effort to reconcile Christianity and Hinduism in his songs. Other poets attempted to express their feelings in songs and hymns. In a telling statement, Macnicol states that the difference between their songs and Tilak's is that "he sang as an Indian poet while they echoed the foreigner ..."

The works of India's Christian *Bhakti* poets were expressed in writings of devotion and theology especially for the Indian Church. These Christian lyrics, whether in song or poetry, were comparable to the Latin hymns of the early Church, to Luther's chorales, to the German hymnodists Gerhardst, Tersteegen and Neander, and to the hymns of the Wesley family and those of Watts in England. There were clear theological expositions in the poetry, as well as simple analogical language of Christian devotion. Many of the poets had comparatively little knowledge of English, and this was attributable in enabling them to clarify their ideas first, the result of which enabled them to speak in a language familiar to their listeners.

The many lyrics reveal a warm, personal approach to God through Christ. God is Lord, King, Guru, Saccidananda, Swami, Ocean of Mercy, Mother and Father. The same terms apply to Christ. The Holy Spirit is spoken of as a flood of joy, medicine for the heart, the key to heaven, the oil of happiness, sacred milk and the Triple Mount or the Holy Trinity.

Where missionaries had not been very successful in endeavouring to build an integrated Indian Christian church, the *Bhakti* poets made Christianity "at home" in India. Their inspiring songs were sung and their poems learnt by thousands who would never read a book on theology. These Christian lyrics, as they were called, were to overshadow the translations of Western hymns, and Bishop Leslie Brown firmly believed that India's Christian lyrical tradition would one day be discovered as a classical contribution to the world's literature[48].

---

48 *Personal communication (October 1999). The Right Rev. Leslie Brown was the first and last English Archbishop of Uganda, Rwanda and Burundi (1961-65), and on his return to England was Bishop of the diocese of St Edmundsbury and Ipswich. Before that he had volunteered to work in India with the Church Missionary Society and was sent to Kerala. He was on the staff of two Theological colleges at Kottayam and Trivandrum and was one of the creators of the Church of South India, inaugurated in St George's Cathedral, Madras. He was fluent in Malayalam, Luganda as well as other languages. Although his Eucharistic Liturgy of the CSI was strongly criticised by some traditional Anglican clergy, it was welcomed by continental Roman Catholic scholars such as Father Louis Bouyer and became one of the sources for the new Vatican II Mass and other modern liturgies such as the New Zealand liturgy. He also worked closely with Bishop Lesslie Newbigin who was CSI Bishop of Madras.*

Next to the Bible, the works of these two poets have been effective and have encouraged the Indian Christian Church to consolidate its functions in India. The lyrics were also to have an influence on the rich musical results inculcated in its worshippers, and were inculturated into the liturgies of the Indian Church[49].

---

49 *See S. Duncan's thesis on the Inculturation of Bhajans in the RC Church in India.*

CHAPTER SIX

Characteristics of the *Bhajan* used in Christian Worship:
Music and Form

The inculturation of the *bhajan* into the Christian liturgy was successful because the musical style was suitable for group worship. Being short and simple, the phrases were easily learnt and the repetition of verses in the leader-chorus style were ideal for singing at large gatherings. In this manner four or five new devotional or worship songs could be learnt at a *kirtana* or a *satsang*. There was a strong urge to equate the music of the Hindu *bhajan* to a style with which missionaries were more familiar in order to disseminate the Christian Gospel. In the nineteenth century, missionaries simply translated Western hymns into Hindi and attempted to adapt words to fit local tunes. It was felt that the Indian monodic style of singing, as in the short phrases of music in the *bhajan*, could be used for Christian worship; however, the uncomfortable absence of European-style counterpoint and harmony needed to be addressed. There followed periods of trial and error, where adaptations of some concepts of Western music to be used in the *bhajan* for Christian worship would be allowed. This was seen as a continuation of a process of inculturation where the Hindu culture first appropriated and absorbed elements from other races and cultures that had made the sub-continent their home by invasion, migration or by other means. It followed that this phase of musical inculturation became a natural progression for the birth of a newer Christian Indian culture to absorb musical elements from Christian Europe.

In order to understand the singing of *bhajans* with substituted Christian texts, which were influenced by Western attitudes and which survived to be developed from a call-and-response style to that of the hymn-type or worship song, it is necessary to examine certain musical features that were conducive to this change. The singing of the *bhajan* in Christian worship centres on certain musical elements:

1. The range of the melody;

2. The melodic structure;

3. The drone and its harmonic implications;

4. Rhythm

1. The Range of the Melodic Line

The melodic structure of the Indian classical melodies stays within the well-defined limits of the Indian scale or *raga*. The *raga* was the structural tune in which the artiste was supposed to perform. As an architect built an edifice around a structural framework, so did the musician, who executed his music work creatively within the framework of the *raga*. The structural melody was maintained so it was discernible at every moment, even with all ornamentations (Music example 2). Rather than apply the term scale, a *raga* could be defined as a combination of notes presenting a melody-like scale pattern. This *raga* pattern was introduced in an ascending *(aroha)* and descending *(avroha)* sequence played on the sitar or the portable harmonium as an introduction.

Music example 2: *Raga Kalyan*

Each *raga* had its own emotional appeal, which alluded to the seasons, and each was played at the appropriate time of the day. Orthodox musicians in India would never play a *raga* except at its proper time of the day or evening. Like the Western monodic tradition, which was originally monastic with the seven-fold timings of the daily liturgies (Matins, Lauds, Tierce, Sext, Nones, Vespers and Compline) and later reduced to five hours in the Latin Liturgy of the Hours (the Office of Readings, Morning Prayer, Daytime Prayer, Evening Prayer and Night Prayer), so too were the seven-fold timings for worship in Hindu temples[50]. This was no new phenomenon. In the Judaic religion mention is made of the division of Psalms into evening, midnight and early morning according to groups for the night watches:

> The nightly study of the Bible can now be traced back to …
> where the following rule, binding to all members of the
> Qumran sect, is found:
>
> "The brothers of the community shall watch together a
> third part of all nights of the year reading from The Book,
> expounding the Law and praying together"
> (Scarfe 1999, 93).

---

50 *Various sources differ in their interpretations of the divisions of worship
in Hinduism. Duncan divides the cycle of the day into eight praharas or
watches, Popley into six periods, and Jenni into seven.*

Divisions of the day for worship in Hinduism, Judaism, Christianity and Islam continued through the centuries. McKinnon notes that St Anthony directs his followers for evening and morning to "sing psalms before sleep and after sleep". During the twentieth century, in the Roman Catholic liturgy in India, *bhajans* were composed which used specific *ragas* relating to the divine hours. Following the reforms of Vatican II, the psalms in the Psalter were divided over four weeks and were to be sung at particular times, for example, Psalms 94 (95), 99 (100) for Morning Prayer, Psalms 4, 90, (91), 133 (134) at Compline.

It is important to recall India's relationship with the Persian, Greek and Arabian empires, with whom she communicated through trade, as their musical systems appear to have an affinity with hers[51]. Some musicologists point to two Greek scales, the Mixolydian and the Doric, as being similar to two Indian scales. Although tenuous, it is indicative of the cultural interchange of musical ideas which may have occurred between the two nations[52].

The *ragas* consisted of seven pitches or *svara*, each of which had a name similar to the sol-fa system. In Jairazbhoy's study many of the *ragas* had their counterparts in Western mediaeval Ecclesiastical modes[53].

---

51 *Recent scholarship points to Greeks and Indians who resided in the Persian Empire, which acted as an intermediary host for trade and exchange of ideas. The Persians also extended the Royal Road to allow for convenient travel. Like the ragas, the Greeks had their modes, the Persians their dastgahs, the Arabs their maquams, all of which were non-harmonic music.*

52 *In some Indian art, which appealed to the Victorians, there appeared to be evidence of Greek, Roman, Byzantine and even Christian influences.*

53 *The ancient Greek modes were named differently, just as the ancient Indian or Sanskrit ragas were also (see Jairazbhoy, page 55). The codification of the Church Modes was probably made in the eighth century, based on the tonal aspect of Gregorian chant.*

Figure 9: *Indian and European Modes*

Svara	Mode	Modern Indian	Ecclesiastical
Sa	C	Bilava	Ionian
Re	D	Kafi	Dorian
Ga	E	Bhairavi	Phrygian
Ma	F	Kalyan	Lydian
Pa	G	Khamaj	Mixolydian
Dha	A	Asavari	Aeolian
Ni	B		Locrian

In Western musicology these modes developed into scales, taking the natural scale beginning on the note C as the standard. According to Duncan, the *Bilaval thatt,* or mode on which the *Bilaval ragas* are based, is similar to the Western diatonic scale. Other ragas based on the *Bilaval thatt* include *Raga Bhupali* and *Raga Jansamohini.*

Music example 3: *Bilaval Thatt*

Duncan's splendid research on the families of *ragas* based on individual *thatts*, which were commonly used in *bhajans* and which therefore led to their being useful to Christian worship, include:

Raga Bilaval;

Raga Kalawati;

Ragas based on the Bhairav thatt;

Ragas based on the Kafi thatt;

Ragas based on the Asavari thatt;

Ragas based on the Bhairavi thatt.

Many of these *ragas* were pentatonic and heptatonic[54], and the melodic range of the *bhajan* had similar characteristics of some folk melodies:

(a) The tonic may be placed at the centre; the melody begins from a note below the tonic, to two or three notes above it;

(b) The tonic may be the lowest note;

(c) The melody may begin in the upper part of the voice and continue by a leap and move to the tonic;

(d) Some notes move in a conjunct way with the second phrase being sung higher;

(e) A phrase may begin at a low register followed by another phrase a sixth above.

The octave range of the melody in the Western diatonic scale appeared to match that of the well-defined limits of the Indian *raga*. It was a template that was appropriated in order to compose melodies for new Christian *bhajans*. To alleviate some of the dullness of the melody imposed by the confines of the *raga*, certain measures were introduced into the Christian *bhajan*. This was the beginning of a distinctly Western style of *bhajan* sung in Christian worship

2. The Melodic Structure

There is a distinct possibility that Christianity, having been born in the Middle East, would have travelled with musical influences from the East and maybe from as far away as India. Embellishment in Indian monody by the singer was undertaken in a similar yet different way, very much as in early European Christianity. Music in the early church was passed down orally.

---

54 *Pandit Bhatkhande, the early twentieth century theorist, proposed ten basic thatts from which all ragas could be derived – Kalyan, Bilaval, Khamaj, Bhairav, Poorvi, Marva, Kafi, Asavari, Bhairavi and Todi thatts.*

Melodies were altered through careless practice or deliberate performance. It was not until the middle of the twelfth century that a system of symbols was invented which indicated pitch, but not the time values of pitch.

Music example 4: *Aeterna Christi munera*

In its developmental style for music in the church, the liturgical plainsong setting of one contrapuntal line, the *cantus firmus*, acted as the melody, while other voices weaved contrapuntal figuration or imitation around it:

Music example 5: *In Nomine by John Taverner (1495-1545)*
(*cantus firmus* is in the alto)

In early European Christian chants, the cantor's phrase would be responded to by a different phrase. The embellishment of melodic figures in early Western monody by highly specialised vocal masters or priest-cantors and their choirs seemingly bears points of contact with the richly developed system of the Indian *gamaka* system[55]. However, in singing the Hindu *bhajan,* there was a distinct lack of the complex ornamentation found in other sacred Indian music. In the singing of the *bhajan*, the *sadhu* or holyman having chanted a phrase, the assembly then repeated it. This had to be simple, as repeating a highly ornamental phrase would certainly be a difficult undertaking for a large group of people singing together. In the Roman Church, the chanting by cantors and their choirs was a means to leading worship – the assembly, though present, did not participate; their worship was of a passive nature.

During the pre-Classical history of music in Europe, both composer and performer recognized various notational and rhythmic conventions. Danielou, Popley, Jenni and others were of the opinion that some of those same features of the *gamak* system could be equated to European ornamentation:

1. The kampita ahata is one of the most effective ornaments in Indian music which may be likened to the appoggiatura and which acted as a delaying note. Also called the humpitam, the appoggiatura or leaning note, Popley wrote, was a note which was not played in the actual raga melody, but suddenly appeared and often. From a European perspective it helped in the flattening or sharpening of notes and tended to fill a blank caused by a lack of harmony.

2. Jenni cites the kampita-gamaka as being comparable to the quilisma (trill from above), while Danielou cites the acciccatura as its equivalent.

---

55 *Jenni (1996): "What interests me about the confrontation is rather what the subtle intricacies of South Asian raga theory suggest with respect to re-examining and reclassifying the (early) Western chant repertory, ill-served by the oversimplification of applying Greek notions of a eight-note system. The misfit is felt most strongly in those ancient pieces whose structural features are at odds with modal theory, and which calls for transposition in order to be notated in the gamut i.e. located such that the odd semitone can be included – or executed." - Personal Communication.*

3. Other notes are emphasised by a kind of bleating (repercussion).
4. The lina produces tonal shadings through pitch-glide and consonant resonance, not unlike the technique called liquescence or "melting".
5. Vali or mida, ripples or slides, are produced by differing techniques.
6. The flurry tiripa or hillola may be the equivalent of the mordent.

Ornaments in the *gamak* system were an integral feature of Indian monody, just as embellishments were in the performance of music during the Renaissance and Baroque periods of European music history. Speaking about Melismatic chanting, Frances Burgess describes:

"This species as undoubtedly Oriental in origin, as it is in character; it was invented in the East, not in the West, and its roots certainly lie in the pre-Christian age … this kind of Plainsong was adapted to Latin and was gradually simplified in the process of Latinlization. It certainly was not a development of the syllabic type of Plainchant for the two kinds existed side by side from the earliest times …" (Hughes, 1996:55)

Some features of the *gamak* system were retained by missionaries who thought of them as being similar to European mordents, turns and passing notes. In the singing of the Christian *bhajan,* embellishments also may appear as a vocal inflection in pitch. Besides adopting the less complex nature of the Hindu *bhajan*, the exceptionally simple performance of the *bhajan* in Christian worship may have also evolved because of the introduction of the portable harmonium. It had been observed that the introduction of this instrument forfeited any complex ornamentation inherent in India's classical music. Commonly used ornaments heard in Christian Indian liturgical music are:

1. The appoggiatura;
2. The turn;
3. The "passing" note;
4. A glissando.

In the following solos some nuances of *gamak* features are heard in the simple tunes of the Christian *bhajan*[56].

Song 2: *Karo meri sahay, Masihaji – Come to my assistance, Lord*[57]

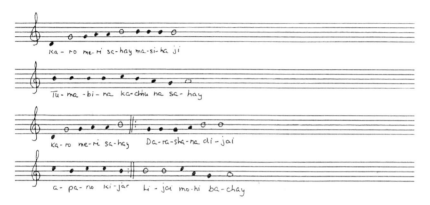

Song 3: *Yahova ki hamd ho – Praise the Lord*

Yahova ki hamd ho	I praise you O Lord my God
Yahova kaa dhanya ho	I bless you, the living One
man merra pyaasaa hai	With all of my heart I seek your face
Parmeshvar tere liye.	My soul thirsts for your love.
Jab bhi mai tere paas aataa hu	Whenever I come to you
mushkile mai apani laataa hu (2)	And bring my troubles before you

---

56 *All music recordings are by the author except where stated, and permission has been given. Due to intonation of singers, notated music may vary.*

57 *Lyrics and musical example, p.106*

aankhe milaakar, mujhe kahate ho	You look at me and say
Aaraam dugaa tere bojh uthaakar	I will give you rest by
	taking your burden.
Jab bhi mai tujhe bulaataa hu	Whenever I cry to you
Dil me mai tujhe bithataa hu (2)	And place you in my heart
Haath pakad kar, mujhe kahate ho	You hold me by the hand
	and say
Hamesha ke liye tere paas rahugaa	I will be with you forever.

(Words by Asha Bhatia; music by Malcolm Ranjore)

Hindi Text

यहोवा की हम्द हो, यहोवा का धन्य हो
मन मेरा प्यासा है, परमेश्वर तेरे लिये

I praise you, O Lord my God,
I bless you, the living one
With all of my heart I seek your face,
My soul thirsts for your love

यहोवा की हम्द हो, यहोवा का धन्य हो
मन मेरा प्यासा है, परमेश्वर तेरे लिये

जब भी मैं तेरे पास आता हूँ
मुश्किले मैं अपनी लाता हूँ
आँखे मिलाकर, मुझे कहते हो
आराम दूंगा तेरा बोझ उठाकर

जब भी मैं तुझे बुलाता हूँ
दिल में मैं तुझे बीठाता हूँ
हाथ पकड़ कर, मुझे कहते हो
हमेशा के लिये तेरे पास रहूंगा

The lines of the *bhajan*, sung with grace notes by the leader, were repeated by the congregation and, if simple enough, also with other ornaments which produced glides. These movements around a single pitch developed from the Hindu *bhajan* and were maintained as being essential to the performing style in the Indian tradition. This practice may have been intuitive in the Indian psyche, as well as learnt.

In Song 4 a simple ornamental phrase is heard, sung by male and female vocalists who are accompanied by a portable harmonium and the *dholak*.

Song 4: *Advent Song*

Introduction:

The one who was to come in the manger,
Has come now as a Saviour,
Being in the form of a babe, a Saviour has come.

1. Jesus has come through the clouds with flashing of lights.
   He came with the Trinity song of salvation.

2. The angels gave glad tidings to the shepherds in the fields,
   Jesus has come to the stable.

3. The prophecies [which were not completed by others.
   Jesus has accomplished]

4. He revealed to everyone the signs of life,
   Made everyone a happy person in fellowship.

5. The message of salvation my Saviour has given,
   Now we are repeating the same message of salvation.

   (Translation by B Robinson)

3. The Drone and its Harmonic implications

Without the drone the singer would feel "like a ship without a rudder" (Popley: page 93). The sound of the drone consolidated the melodic line and provided a background support. Each *raga* was accompanied by a drone:

Music example 6: *Raga melodies & drones*

The drone was played on the *tambura*, the strings of which were tuned to the fundamental note and the fifth, or sometimes the fourth. This was often reinforced by the *sruti-patti* or pitch box, an organ-like instrument on which no tune was played; only a single drone chord or note was continually sounded. This modal perception existed by the relationship of the notes to each other and especially to the fundamental note or "tonic". The prevailing note or the "dominant" was always present in the background or was continually sounded with the tonic as a drone. Because of this effect, the accompaniment of chords I and V in European harmony appeared to be a neat solution to the singing of the *bhajan* in Christian worship in India and its diaspora. In this respect, the introduction of the portable harmonium used as an accompanying instrument was a "godsend" to missionaries and others concerned with Christian worship.

Although the singing of the melodic line remains almost the same as it was sung in India, the drone is absent in the *bhajans* sung in Christian worship in islands of the diaspora due to the use of other melodic instruments[58].

In major cities in England and the Americas, and to some extent on the sub-continent of India, experiments in contemporary music pertaining to the sounding of the drone can be heard in

---

58 *The influence of Trinidad's other types of music, such as calypso, soca and chutney-calypso appear to have no influence on the style of singing the bhajan as they have had on the performance of Western style worship songs.*

the following extract. There is an attempt to integrate the drone into the accompaniment played on the guitar, which also plays the *raga* pattern.

Song 5:1 *Deep Jale (solo)*[59]

In the same song played by the group OLIO with sitar and tabla, the drone is heard as an accented note.

Song 5:2 *Deep Jale (group)*

Keep the lamp burning	Deep jale
so the Lord's name	Prabhu naam rahe
Will remain, will remain in the temple	Mere mandir mein
Remain in my heart.	Mandir mein.
In the morning and in the evening	Saanj sabere ye man gaaye
My soul sings to you	Yesu teraa naam
Jesus your name	Prabhu Yesu teraa naam
Lord Jesus, your name	Naam rahe man mein
Let your name	Prabhu naam rahe
Remain in my soul	Man mein.
Lord, for your name to dwell in me.	

Harmony can be assessed in different ways. As mentioned earlier, every tone in the melody has to agree with the fundamental note directly and to the fourth or fifth. There appears to be a linear approach to harmony through the harmonic structures of each note, to those of other notes, to phrases, and the continuous musical phrases of the *bhajan*. Another interpretation of the term harmony in the performance of the *bhajan*, is the sense of togetherness endorsed in singing as a group. Bake had recognised the fact that singing in unison or of the octave produces its own

---

59 *Chris and his group have encouraged many South Asian musicians in England to compose and perform music for the liturgy with very successful results. The words and music of Deep Jale are by Anil Dev, and the arrangement is by Peter Hicks and Chris Hale.*

"harmony" in Indian music[60]. The three vocal registers bear a resemblance to those of European music and can be conceived in the following ways as:

1. The low octave, the equivalent to the bass register;

2. The middle octave, the equivalent to the tenor and alto voices;

3. The high octave or the treble voice.

The harmony of combining voices in three octaves has a powerful appeal in Indian music and it is in the *kirtan* or hymn recital where this sense of harmony is maintained and keenly conveyed, as in Song 4. In the Christian *bhajan*, with its simple melodic line following the European triadic harmony and accompanied with the harmonic chords I and V, the need for complex rhythms on hand drums was usurped. What the accompanying drums can be seen to have added was a sense of vitality to a melodic style of singing which had lost its complex improvisationary elements due to the introduction of the portable harmonium and other Western melodic instruments. It was a way of keeping the drum players as musicians within the Christian community.

4. Rhythm

Musical time in traditional Indian music was seen as a development from ancient prose and metres of poetry. The complex uses of rhythmic patterns or *talas* were awkward to use in the performance of the Christian *bhajan,* which had acquired the accompaniment of chordal harmony; therefore, the rhythmic cyclic patterns performed in Indian traditional music were abandoned[61]. Karolyi talks of Indian rhythm as being additive,

60 *An interesting parallel is in McKinnon, where he writes of [Saint] Anthony figuratively speaking of harmony as "not only the low sounds, but combined with middle and high sounds, all blend together in balanced tension".*

61 *A collector and arranger of Indian songs for the harpsichord, William*

Tambur (Photo Gilda Sebastin)

that is, rhythm in Indian classical music is a concept of duration; long and short beats are organised in patterns repeated in different

Hamilton Bird in 1789, complained that he was at great pains to add a form of key signature "which the music of Hindostan is extremely deficient in." (in Clayton, page 5).

units throughout a piece. Philip Glass, the American composer who has experimented with Indian rhythms, explains his thinking of the different concepts in the following words:

In Western music we divide time – as if you were to bake a length of time and slice it the way you slice a loaf of bread. In Indian music … you take small units, or "beats" and string them together to make up larger time values.

Just as the *raga* denoted a system of melodic organisation, so the concept of the *tala* (*tal* or measure of time) may be referred to as a system of rhythmic organisation[62]. A *tala* comprises a set number of beats or *matras* which are divided into cycles; for example, a *dadra tala* has six *matras* in each unit, and the first beat is accented:

Figure 10: *The Dadra Tala*

1 2 3 4 5 6 / 1 2 3 4 5 6 / etc.

In the performance of the music, hand signals were used to indicate the main beat and the sub-divisions of a section or *vibhag* – the *sama* is the main beat; the *tali* the minor beats; and the *kali* the silent beat or rest. These recurring rhythmic patterns, *talas*, can be several bars (according to the Western concept) with different time signatures. An example of this additive effect of the *Dhamar tala* is illustrated:

Figure 11: *The Dhamar Tal*

---

62 *The term, tal, may be equated to time measure conceived as a cycle – (1) quantitative, the duration of a cycle measured in beats at three tempi and (2) qualitative, the distribution of accents in the cycle.*

The *Tintal* cycle with sixteen beats is the most frequently used *tala* for many *bhajans* and consists of four *matras* per *vibhag*. It appears that Indian rhythms defied missionaries and other Westerners. A simple option was the use of the *Tintal tala*, which could be transcribed easily to 4/4 time and 2/4 time[63].

In conjunction with rhythm, tempo cannot be ignored. Three basic tempi or *laya(s)* are recognised – a slow tempo or *vilambit*, a moderate tempo or *madhyam*, and a fast tempo or *drut*. In the singing of *bhajans* the moderate tempo is used frequently, with the cantor or leader switching to the faster tempo and back.

With the advent of Protestant missionaries in India during the nineteenth century, the European concept of chordal harmony was employed. The accompaniment using chord I and chord V appeared to echo successfully the sounds of the fundamental tone and the prevailing tone in the Indian *raga*. The simplicity of the melodic line of the Hindu *bhajan* paved the way for the adoption of singing the *bhajan* in Christian worship. Where the *gamak* system was concerned, it may be deduced that some musical aspects were retained by missionaries[64] who appropriated European musical theory to assist in their tasks of composing *bhajans* as a tool for evangelization and for the new converts to use in Christian worship.

The newly created type of *bhajans* for Christian worship sung by the early converts in the British colonial islands in the Caribbean, Fiji and Mauritius were sung from memory, continuing the oral tradition of *parampara*, the guru/pupil relationship

---

63 *If, however, one begins to examine the Christian worship songs sung in India and its diaspora, although the bhajans have adopted 2/4 or 4/4 time, their counterpart in the form of the Muslim quawali and ghazal is usually in a slightly faster rhythm of 3/8 or 6/8. Music played in the courts of Muslim invaders was of a lively disposition. Many holy men adopted the structure of the Hindu bhajan but, it could be said, retained their style of music.*

64 *Roman Catholic missionaries made use of this and only later did the Protestants adopt the idea.*

from India. It was a continuation from a culture where oral transmission effectively espoused careful "composition" and precise memorisation. Because of the type of oral tradition, hours of continuous singing in a *kirtan* or hymn recital, where many *bhajans* were learnt, were not unusual. The singing of *bhajans* in this situation was eventually to promote congregational singing and the full active participation of the assembly.

The musical call-and-response form of the *bhajan* which was used in Christian worship falls into two categories, direct repetition and the Litany pattern.

1. Direct repetition

Many *bhajans* sung in early Christian worship were strophic, with refrains of one or two lines; these could be compared with Psalms 46 and 47, which were the forerunners of vast collections of refrain hymns[65]. A non-strophic form, the *nam kirtan*, which is used in Hindu worship and in which several names and epithets of a deity are sung repeatedly, was uncommon in the islands of the diaspora; however, compositions by contemporary artistes have introduced the *nam kirtan* into worship in India and the Americas within a Christian context.

The basic form was typical of the *bhajan,* which was introduced into British colonies by missionaries and brought to Europe and the Americas from India by Christian immigrants. The assembly repeated each line of the music and text sung by the leader:

> Short vocal or instrumental introduction (optional)
> **A**: Leader   **A**: Assembly
> **B**: Leader   **B**: Assembly
> **C**: Leader   **C**: Assembly
> **D**: Leader   **D**: Assembly

---

65 *Dissertation by Scarfe, 1999:90.*

This repetitive type allowed for some variation and the pattern in which the chorus returned after each verse was frequently used. The call-and-response form allowed individuals to learn new *bhajans*, being led by stronger singers and allowing weaker singers to be led. This style of singing the *bhajans* was practised within the Hindu community and this pattern was adhered to in Christian worship.

In the following *bhajan* care was taken in the choice of melody and of the text, as a long text with a difficult melody would be uninviting to the worshipping community.

Song 6 / Music example 7: *Karo meri sahay*

Chorus:

Karo meri sahay,Masihaji	Come to my assistance, Lord
Tuma bina kachhu na sahay.	Without you I can bear nothing.

1. Darashana dijai apano kijai,   1. Give me a vision of Thyself
   darashana dijai apano kijai,   Make me thine own and save me.
   lijai mohi bachay.

2. Yajagako nistarana karana   2. For the world's Salvation
   Janama liyo tuma ay.   wast thou born.

3. Tino dinamen uthe kabaraten   3. After three days you came out of
                         the grave.
   Deshina tain bata ray   To reveal yourself to mankind.

4. Suna lijai Prabhu binati meri,   4. Listen Lord to this my prayer,
   Awaguna pai nahi jay.   Let not evil befall me.[66]

---

66 *Words and translation by Chauharjasingh 1991.*

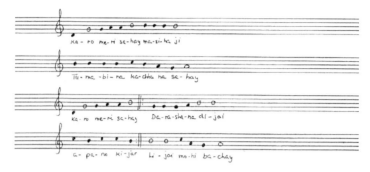

Another variation frequently used was the singing of a *bhajan* which began with an introductory chorus. This was followed by each verse in a repetitive manner and ended with the chorus with which it began. In the repetitive call-and-response *bhajan,* ad hoc versions were improvised where, for example, a new verse could be inserted by an individual to emphasise a theological point of the story or to clarify part of it to the assembled group in the *kirtan.* This entailed much discussion beforehand, and one may imagine the heated arguments that may have ensued[67]. Due to the informality with which the *kirtan* was conducted, any member of the group was free to add his own theological exposition to the Christian storyline. This textual "improvisation" was an accepted part of later established *kirtans.*

For the assembly to know when to rejoin the singing together, one line of the refrain was sung. This "cue" signal could be compared to the cue signal also found in Psalmody (Psalm 66:1-11).

> *Response*: Come now and see the works of God
> who holds our souls in life
>
> Be joyful in God, all you lands;
> sing the glory of his name;
> sing the glory of his praise.
> Say to God, "How awesome are your deeds!
> Because of your great strength
> your enemies cringe before you." *R*

---

67 *Indeed, this is what I remember as a young child in the nightly meetings in Trinidad.*

All the earth bows down before you,
sings to you, sings out your name.
Come now and see the works of God,
How wonderful he is in doing towards all his people. *R*

The cue in the *bhajan* was not only intended for the singers, but would also have been the signal for anyone who was listening to join in, as those who were in attendance may have comprised non-Christians as well as practising Christians who were learning the *bhajan* in Hindi for the first time. This call-and-response form still applies in the learning of a new *bhajan*, especially if it is sung in Hindi in the islands mentioned, and in a *satsang* or "truth-gathering" session in Europe and the Americas. The *satsang* was envisaged mainly as an outreach to non-Christian Asians by Christian Asians.

Since the migrations to other parts of the world from India, the basic structure of the *bhajan* has evolved because of its coming into contact with other cultures. Once the *bhajan* was learnt it was sung by all in unison as a worship song in the form of a hymn and without the call-and-response pattern. However, the repetitive form was kept as a tradition in the *kirtans*. As many of the *bhajans* now sung have evolved into simple worship songs, this facilitates the singing of *bhajans*, not unlike hymns, by the assembly as a whole and applies when a *bhajan* is well-known or popular. The call-and-response mode would have been an apt method of learning the text and the music by untutored people, and even by those who could read, as it was in keeping with a tradition that was maintained. This method of learning was superseded by printed literature, as evidenced when a printing press was built in Trinidad by Rev. Morton, and indeed by missionaries in the then British Commonwealth countries, and as it had been in India. Nevertheless, in Indian communities across the world the concept of memorisation was very much respected and this tradition continued despite the growth of printed literature.

It has emerged that in countries of the diaspora where meetings for single-sex groups have been conducted the call-and-response form is not always adhered to. The *bhajan* at the beginning of the meeting is sometimes sung as a solo (Song 7:1), or as a duet (Song 7:2), in place of a prayer or as a means of meditation. During the meeting it may be sung by everyone or only a small group.

Song 7: *Yesu ne kaha (solo and duet)*

Yesu ne kaha	Jesus, the Lord said,
Jivan ki roti mynhi hun	"I am the bread of life."

Song 8, which is a strophic *bhajan*, is sung by a member of the older generation who used to travel widely in Trinidad teaching *bhajans* to village communities, and to young people, so that the *bhajan* would be remembered and not forgotten.

Song 8: *Fountain of Love (solo)*

Fountain of love, have mercy on us and
Appear unto us.

1. We sin excessively in mind and body
   O Lord, give us your forgiveness.

2. We your servants are totally useless
   Give us the strength to do your bidding.

3. In this ocean of the world uncertainty abounds,
   Day by day do protect your servants[68]

---

68 *It is to Mrs Myna Hussein I owe my thanks for recording this bhajan. Due to her dedication in attempting to teach the younger people the bhajans she remembered we have some of the old songs.*

In worship groups held in churches, house groups or conventions one often hears a *bhajan* being sung by two large groups in the call-and-response mode. This style of antiphonal singing can only be rendered when it could be assumed that the *bhajan* is popular or is well known by the whole community. Other styles of singing have been adopted from European music. A short canon-like style is heard towards the end of Song 9, which begins with a short introduction. Some verses are sung in "harmonic" unison by a mixed group with male and female dividing to sing different verses in which they are accompanied by a portable harmonium, a sitar and tabla.

Song 9: *The Pilot*[69]

Dear Jesus, Thou art merciful and the Creator
We sing praises to you as Thou art the Saviour.

There was darkness everywhere then Thou appeared
Thou bore the cross and took our sins, and through your suffering at the cross, redeemed us.

My boat, like life was in danger, was rocking against the storms
But then Thou guided us as a protector and took us across the stormy journey.

My life was miserable and I was dying to gain salvation from other ways but all in vain.

But soon Thou took mercy upon me, and cared for me, all my sins left me and I became a healthy person again.

---

69 *Songs 9 and 10 have been translated by Benjamin Robinson and his group has recorded this music.*

At the beginning of this *bhajan* (Song 10), there is a call to the Lord for help by the leader. A ground bass melody comes from a cue signal which underscores both the male or the female singing.

Song 10: *Majire mohe*

> Oh! The Captain of my [life] boat,
> It is my request to guide me and help me to cross the river [river of worldly life].
>
> My life is stuck in the whirling water and is stumbling,
> Take me across through this danger.
>
> I am feeble and weak and shaky,
> Come, Thou oh Saviour and row it and take me across this storm.
>
> The sea waves [sinful life style] are very frightening and I am tired coming through the tumult,
> Therefore guide me and take me across.
>
> There is love and greed of money everywhere and everyone wants [to] gain from it
> But oh! Captain of my boat take me through safely.
>
> Thou saved your followers in the stormy lake,
> Save me [also], Saviour and Rock of my boat.

2. The Litany pattern

In this musical form the leader sings a list of phrases and the assembly responds by repeating a refrain or an acclamation. It is possible that this form may have come from work songs, which were quite common in communities which inhabited areas around the rivers or the Malabar coastline of India. Historically, in pre-Hinduism the sacred and the secular were entwined – there was no marked division – and although the singing of songs was an integral facet of ordinary life, a sense of the sacred was realised and maintained. As the actual vocalisation was conceived as an act of worship, this act identified the singer with God through song.

It is conceivable that the litany pattern (Figure 12) may have developed from occupational songs through a call-and-response mode. This form has allowed for many possibilities in text (Figure 13) and has been used extensively in the Roman Catholic liturgy in India, as well as in such communities in England.

Figure 12: *The Litany Pattern*

Introduction - optional

A: Leader   Assembly Response
B: Leader   Assembly Response
C: Leader   Assembly Response
D: Leader   Assembly Response

Coda - optional

Figure 13: *Inculturation of a Litany Response*

Cantor:	**Assembly:**
Cosmic Mind	I call on you
Om Saccidananda	I turn to you
Allah ir-Rachman ir-Rachim	I surrender to you
Sea of Peace	I drink from you
Flame of all loves	I burn with you

This style of the litany is sung in the assemblies where there is a high population of Catholic South Asians. In the following litany, Indian texts have been woven for worship in the Christian liturgy.

Music example 8: *You are my father*[70]

Taizé hymns

The simplicity of the *bhajan,* like the simple Taizé hymns[71], offers a great deal which can be gleaned about the theology which underpins the Christian community. The short repetitive musical phrases and texts allow all to participate as a full assembly, embracing those who are new to the Christian faith as well as visitors. Its development to simple worship songs sung in unison in the West became a musical asset which was easily absorbed into

---

70 *I am indebted to Father J. Wijngaards and Jackie at HOUSETOP, who kindly sang this for me amongst other such litanies and bhajans. I am also thankful for his permission in allowing me to use this particular piece in this work. Dr Wijngaards was born in Holland and studied at the Gregorian University in Rome where he gained a doctorate. His book,* Did Christ Rule Out Women Priests? *argued for women priests and caused quite a stir. He was ordained at Mill Hill in 1959 and had been a theologian with the world-renowned Mill Hill Missionaries, and is a prolific author.*

71 *See Chapter 8, note 76.*

the liturgies of the churches in the Indian diaspora. An interesting aspect was the tendency to revert to the call-and-response format when so desired by worshippers and when the occasion demanded it. For example, this style has been a regular occurrence when celebrating the public holiday Arrival Day in Trinidad. In England the call-and-response style has been used to teach young British Asians a *bhajan* in a particular Indian language, as there are new generations who speak only English. This may apply equally to other communities in the diaspora for their respective uses.

In East Indian communities in the Caribbean, Guyana, Fiji and Mauritius, East African countries and in some parts of South Africa, in addition to Western hymns and simple harmonic worship songs the *bhajan* was maintained as a tradition. In Europe and America a bolder approach was about to break onto the South Asian liturgical music scene, fired by the impact of the popular Asian music circuit.

CHAPTER SEVEN

Instruments in Worship

Historically, it has been argued that the voice as a musical instrument was all that was needed to sing God's praises. An instrument which was used for dance and festivities outside the church was considered profane and not to be used for Christian worship. Another argument against the use of instruments was that the theological Word could not be transmitted, therefore they were unacceptable for worship. The exceptions were bells, which gave aural signals, for example at the elevation of the host in the Mass as well as at baptisms, weddings and funerals. Small and large bells were used in pre-Christian communities for different purposes, and in temples and places of worship in India, finger cymbals were used. Bells passed easily from monastic use to parochial uses; besides summoning the faithful to church they alerted communities to danger in war, fire and storms, or extraordinary meetings.

Many years have passed since missionaries to the sub-continent banned the playing of Indian instruments in Christian worship as they were considered "pagan". It was many centuries prior to that when the playing of indigenous instruments was encouraged and approved of by a missionary. Since then the issue has been debated fiercely. Vatican II and its policy on inculturation within the established Christian doctrine acted as the catalyst in allowing those same instruments to be experimented with in worship and other ritual practices. As an important subject, Sacred Music was given a chapter to itself, wherein instruments were allowed a supporting role. The members of the Council conceded that the organ had acquired a privileged position and that other instruments were complimentary to the liturgy if used in a dignified manner and as an aid to worship. It was recognised that in non-Western cultures the context in which indigenous instruments were to be used for Christian worship was valid so long as these instruments were played in response to the action of the liturgy and enabled the beauty of worship for its worshippers.

Roberto de Nobili (1605), a Jesuit priest, was the notable missionary who was behind the concept of inculturation. Instead of imposing Western ideas on his converts, he joined them by subsuming himself in the local customs. He dressed in saffron robes of a *sanyasi*, a Hindu holy man, ate as the people ate and studied the Vedic and Bhakti literatures. His converts continued to use the *santal*, the mark on the forehead, the *kudumi* badge and the sacred thread, which were expressions of the Brahmin caste. It can be surmised that he may have attempted to integrate local practices and customs further into the domain of the liturgy as Rome and the Portuguese Inquisitor became involved. Eventually, all was decided in de Nobili's favour. Vatican II was to question this same practice and decided to follow de Nobili's stand on inculturation.

R. Qureshi provides an insight to the playing of instruments which were used for musical expression in worship. He describes instruments accompanying a *quawali (bhajan)*:

> The vigorous drum accompaniment on the barrel-shaped dholak is reinforced by hand clapping while the portable harmonium ... underscores the song melody.[72]

In Hinduism, hand-clapping used to accompany the singing – also indicating the clapping away of bad deeds or "sins". The harmonium, which was introduced by the British to India as an accompanying instrument to hymn singing, was viewed as an absurd instrument for use in the Indian culture. To their credit, the South Asian musicians took this instrument and made it their own. It was an incongruity that this instrument was turned into a melodic and drone instrument which could be used with musical integrity in worship by the participants themselves.

In the diaspora the singing of *bhajans* in worship was accompanied by instruments, some of which, like drums, came with the indentured labourers. There was no hesitation about using these instruments, as it assumed a response to a perception of cultural identity first and foremost and by then it was too late to oppose their use in Christian worship. No division was made as to whether the instruments were used for Christian worship or pleasure, as both sacred and secular practices crossed boundaries in the diaspora.

In Trinidad and Tobago the church, as well as employing musical forms from the motherland, also made use of Indian instruments.

> On entering the church we found the men's orchestra of wind, string and percussion instruments in full swing and filling the building with alternately furious climaxes of sound and droning cadences. Eighty men sat cross-legged on the platform on one side of the pulpit following, on their drums, cymbals, flutes and castanets, their leader who led on a huge pair of castanets. The leader kept weaving these intricate patterns in the air and worked up into repeated crescendos, chanting, swaying, jiggling and keeping time

---

72 *In Karolyi, page 139.*

for his companions. The leader led out with the chant and
the others came in with the refrain. This continued for
half an hour, with the congregation deeply absorbed and
the children drinking it in. There followed a forty minute
service, including two poorly rendered hymns. At the
close of the service the orchestra began where it left off.
(Merle, page 37)

In Trinidad and Tobago many of the instruments used to
accompany the *bhajans* are now made locally. The *dholak*, a
double-headed cylindrical drum brought from India, is cut from
the mango tree, and the heads are covered with goat skin. Other
instruments which are also made locally are the *nagara* and the
tassa, which are two types of single clay-bowl drums played in
pairs and played for more social occasions like weddings, which
in themselves followed a pattern of worship. The bronze or brass
idiophones are the *khajri*, a single-headed frame with jingles, and
the *kartal*, wooden clappers with or without jingles. The *dhantal*,
an idiophone, is claimed to be of Indo-Trinidad origin. It is thought
to be a creation of the indentured Indians, but it has been used by
the East Indian communities in Suriname (Dutch Guiana) as well.
Some form may have come with the indentured labourers and
may have evolved to the present structure. According to a local
theory, the long steel rod was adapted from the *danta* or prong
used to connect the yokes of two bullocks which drew the sugar
cane-filled cart on the estate. The curved piece used to strike the
dhantal was a metal horse-shoe used on the estate mules and
horses. In the New World to which the Indian immigrants came
it became an additional instrument for providing rhythm and is
now an important instrument in local music groups, apart from
the East Indian communities.

In Trinidad and Tobago society, any object which is capable of
producing a musical rhythmic sound is co-opted as an "instrument"
and many such oddities are to be found accompanying singing

in general. Copying examples of homemade instruments used at Carnival time, the East Indian communities have followed the same pattern. These "rhythm instruments" may include a *lota* or bronze goblet which is struck with a spoon or a metal "beater", a grater scraped backward and forward with a spoon imitating the sound of a guiro, and even chac-chacs; these were the gourds of the calabash tree which were dried and filled with seeds. The outer dried shells from the seedpods of the mahogany tree were held in one hand and knocked together in the style of playing the castanets.

The *sitar,* which was brought by rich Indians later and used when indentureship ended, and the *veena* appear to be seldom used in Christian worship, if at all. The possibility exists that the *sitar* was also thought of as a labourer's instrument because of past colonialism. Those two instruments have been superseded by modern keyboard instruments or other melodic instruments – electric organs and keyboards, clarinets, saxophones and the piano. One indigenous instrument which is being experimented with is the steelpan, which appears to be used as a solo instrument during worship rather than in accompaniment.

In Great Britain the choice of instruments for Christian worship is dependent on the worshippers. It has been known for instruments of only Indian origin – including the portable harmonium – to be used in a totally South Asian gathering. Frequently, there is the combination of Indian and Western instruments, including clarinets, flutes and the drum kit. No longer is any distinction made in playing instruments for worship or leisure in the diaspora; nevertheless, it depends on the particular worshipping assembly as to what instruments or groups of instruments are available or required.

As the Church was born into a particular culture, and its development was rooted in different cultures, the East Indians and South Asians in the Indian diaspora saw no reason why their instruments should not be used with integrity in Christian worship. The use of this mixture of Eastern, Western and local instruments where they settled was to become a rich and growing source for the Christian liturgy.

Portable Harmonium (Photo Gilda Sebastin)

Sitar Students (photo Gilda Sebastin)

Sarangi (Photo Gilda Sebastin)

Murili gourd pipe (Photo Gilda Sebastin)

Tabla (Photo Gilda Sebastin)

Midrigam (Photo Gilda Sebastin)

Bamboo Flute, also called Bansuri (c Gilda Sebastian)

Dhantal from Trinidad (photo HJN)

CHAPTER EIGHT

Sing to the Lord a New Song
Psalm 149:1

The *bhajan* as sung in the Land of Bharat travelled with immigrants in the Indian diaspora, and in the case of Trinidad and Tobago, Mauritius and Fiji it was also introduced to those islands by missionaries.

Musically, it has been seen that there are in existence in India and Europe what are essentially tone systems built on seven-degree scales that have names and are associated with the sol-fa system. Both classical systems place emphasis on the first and fifth degrees of the scale or *raga*, its fundamental tone or tonic and the prevailing tone or dominant. The result of European harmony, which contrasted with an amended simple Indian melodic system, was an important outcome in music performance by Indian Christian worshippers. Since there are seemingly numerous points of similarity, a syncretic form could be expected to have evolved. The social relationship between societies, changes in attitudes and the general evaluation of worship music were important in determining what compatibilities of stylistic elements were involved.

The official sanction of both Catholic and Protestant hierarchies no longer holds the tremendous sway it did in earlier times when indigenous music and dance and the associated arts were frowned upon. Many lay assemblies now determine their own direction within a truly Christian theological context. In music, Christians of the East Indian communities in ex-colonial islands have tended to select Western models for their liturgical repertoire. This is not surprising, as the descendants of the indentured migrants are European in outlook and, in the case of Trinidad and Tobago, American influenced. Musical ideas generated on the Spanish, Australian and African mainlands, as well as from jazz, rock and pop traditions, are gradually influencing worship among the younger generation, much to the annoyance of some of the older generation. This interesting mix or fusion can no longer be viewed according to the old term of inculturation. There is perhaps a perception of what can be termed revitalisation, which perhaps indicates an unleashing of creative styles that are continually reformed. No longer does Merriam's theory hold true that "less change can be expected in religious than in social or recreational music".

Although the singing of the *bhajan* in Christian worship in churches had elapsed over a period of time, it was nevertheless kept alive by older folk at house venues and in *kirtans*. There were also peripatetic services to communities who wished Christian *bhajans* to be sung at various ceremonies and who wanted to learn these sacred songs so that they would not be forgotten. Individuals took it upon themselves to imbue a sense of belonging to a community by teaching and singing these *bhajans*. In recent years there has been a revival in the Christian community of learning and singing *bhajans*. This has arisen as a counter-measure to young Hindus who show a great delight and enthusiasm in singing their own *bhajans* (influenced by the importation of films from India), as indeed it has been with the Muslim sector in singing their devotional songs. It is also an effort to re-establish the fact that *bhajans* were originally a Hindu concept and not a Christian innovation, and that it was part of Hindu ritual and practice long before Christian worship established them as part of the liturgy for church services. Of course, there has been no claim that it was Christian orientated by the churches, so there has never been any kind of challenge. In the churches and their environs there appears to be a deliberate exchange and change of musical awareness from both Hindus and Christians. It remains a matter of pride and mutual respect among the communities of both Hindus and Christian Indians so that there is no room for resentment or controversy. These causal changes are seen as a respectful exchange of worship music and as a perception of cultural identity.

A question frequently posed is whether the musical style of the *bhajan* has retained an Indian quality. This is sometimes difficult to define. A significant factor is the influence of all styles of sacred music, as well as popular music – including recent influxes of music from around the world. It could be surmised that because of these influences the response from the East Indian communities in the diaspora and South Asians in Europe and America is an attempt to preserve, or to maintain, sometimes even to abandon, and, furthermore, an attempt to syncretise musical traditions. As a result of these tendencies, liturgical music in the Indian diaspora is in a state of unprecedented diversity. Where *bhajans* are sung in Christian worship, the Indian-ness appears to resemble nuances in intonation. This, in the view of the local communities, is an attempt to maintain an Indian-ness through some likely form of ornamentation which may be ascertained by movements around a single pitch or slides between pitches. A guarded attempt to keep the form and simple style of the *bhajan* in Christianity has met with some success. In publications the lyrics of *bhajans* are written in Hindi, and, almost always, there is a transliteration into Romanised

Hindi as well as a translation of what is being sung. Some of these *bhajans* are published in the worship song books along with hymns from European and American sources. The term *bhajan* appears to be interchangeable with the term hymn, and is also used for the call-and-response form when sung in Hindi.

The use of terms denoting *bhajan* is in an exploratory phase. Many South Asian Christians in England prefer to use the term "Indo-Christian worship song", sometimes leaving out the prefix "Indo" or substituting "South Asian". Some Europeans, on the other hand, recognise the fact that they are worship songs of and from the Indian sub-continent and the diaspora and refer to them as Indian Christian lyrics.

In Great Britain, unlike Trinidad and Tobago, there appears to be a psychological barrier to using the form and the music of the *bhajan* – and even the term, where the first and second migrant generations are concerned, especially if they have been converts to Christianity.

Recollection of the theological connotation of the Hindu *bhajan* is still too recent for comfort; therefore, the direction in worship veers towards more Western hymns and worship songs. The dependence on and performance of this repertoire is perhaps an indication to friends, families and fellow worshippers of their total acceptance of Christianity. It is only after a long period that converts who feel secure in their beliefs are able to re-assess the *bhajan* for use in Christian worship.

Interestingly, in England many are unaware of a reverse situation in which the words of Mother Teresa's *Peace Prayer* were taken from the Upanishads[73].

---

73 *The tradition that St Thomas had visited a Parthian king of Ghandhara has been suggested by James Fergusson, who also thought that Christian elements appeared in the Bhagavad Gita, (in Keay, page 145).*

> Lead me from death to life
> From falsehood to truth,
> Lead me from despair to hope,
> From fear to trust.
> Lead me from hate to love,
> From war to peace.
> Let peace fill our heart, our world,
> Our universe.

The music was composed by Donald Swann and is sung as a canon and in the response/call form of a *bhajan*[74]. In the islands of the diaspora, especially in Trinidad and Tobago, this poem is frequently quoted in worship.

The influence of various styles in contemporary worship music is seen in the innovative experiments in composition which are being pursued by British musicians and younger generations of British Asians[75].

Hilary Brown has composed "I Am/*Main Haan*", sung as a solo and accompanied on a keyboard in lieu of the portable harmonium. She uses the style of the *bhajan,* which also could be sung in a repetitive fashion or as a worship song by a group.

Song 11: *I Am / Main Haan (Punjabi)*

Chorus:

> Ikk aad mee nay per may shur noon puchiaa, Tay raa naam kee hai?
> Tay per may shur oos noon kayaa, Main haan jo main haan.

> A man one day requested God, "Who are you, what is your name?"
> And God replied, "This is my name, I Am who I Am."

---

74 *In* Come and Praise 2, *1992: 140.*

75 *These songs were performed at the first competition of Asian Christian Music (the first of its kind), at which the author adjudicated. Permission was kindly given to me to use the following: Nos. 10,.11, 12, 13, 14, 15.*

1. In the beginning was the word   Aad vich shabad see.
   The Word became flesh.   Shabad day daa ree hoyeeaa.
   And lived with us,   Tay saa day vich vaas keetaa,
   His name is Jesus.   Oos daa naam yesoo hai.

Chorus

2. Jesus said,   Yesoo nay kayaa,
   "I am the Light of the world."   Jugat daa chaanan main haan."
   Jesus is the radiance of   Per may shur day mehimaa daa
   God's glory.   Yesoo vich pergat hai.

Chorus

3. Jesus said,   Yesoo nay kayaa,
   "I am the Bread of life   "Jee van dee rotee main hain."
   The one who feeds on me   Jiraa menoo khaan daa hai
   will live because of me."   oh mayray kaaran jee vay gaa."

Chorus

4. Jesus said,   Yesoo nay kayaa,
   "I am the resurrection   "Pooran ootaan tay jeevan
   and the life.   main haan.
   He who believes in me   Jo may ray ootay nichaa kardaa
   he will live."   hai, oh sadaa jee vay gaa."

Chorus

Another example of a composition sung in both English and Hindi is a vocal piece by Chris and Doug Fekete. The accompaniment is played on the guitar and the *dholak*. The chorus in "All Good Gifts" could be sung by a group, repeated in *bhajan* fashion.

Song 12: *All Good Gifts – Uske nam*

Chorus	Chorus
All good gifts they come from God Ask and you shall receive them All good gifts they come from God Ask in the name of Jesus.	Uske nam me preme hai Uske nam me kushi hai Uske nam me daya hai Tarif ho yesu nam ki.
1. There is love in His name There is joy in His name There is mercy in His name Praise the name of Jesus.	1. Uske nam me shanti hai Uske nam me asha hai Uske namme aram hai Tarif ho Yesu nam ki.
Chorus	Chorus
2. There is peace in His name There is hope in His name There is rest in His name Praise the name of Jesus.	2. Uske nam me takat hai Uske nam me shifa hai Uske nam me shakti hai Uske ho Yesu nam ki.
Chorus	Chorus

The last line acts as a cue signal to the assembly to join in the chorus.

There are young South Asians who have also seen the need to compose for the society of which the Indian culture is an important part. Palo Parkash's composition "Beloved, be courageous" is performed by a small group of singers who are accompanied by a portable harmonium, a tabla and dholak. This is in a strophic *bhajan* style.

Song 13: *Beloved, be courageous – Piero himat vando*

Chorus

Beloved, be courageous, move forward
Take the sign of the cross,
Friends, we will win and Satan will loose.

1. Fight, fight diligently, Jesus is captain,
    Be courageous, keep hope, Satan will flee.

2. In sin and suffering all around, people are dying
    Be merciful towards the world and they [will be] surprised.

3. Go to every house and be witnesses of Christ
    Because He is King of salvation, merciful towards everyone.

4. Quickly say to everyone, words of Jesus
    Sinners are being saved, those who put their trust in Him.

5. The writer says, [the] enemy is ashamed when they hear of Jesus
    People are believing in Christ, and Satan is loosing.

The above three examples, which imitate the form and style of the *bhajan*, also lend themselves to congregational rendition, and in all the songs the theological aspect is succinctly made. Although the call-and-response form was not a unique idiom to the *Bhakti* movement, this method was successful in filling a requirement where theology was concerned. By repeating short phrases the theology of Christianity was learnt by the masses who attended *kirtans or satsangs*. This performance practice was essential, especially to new converts.

There is also a growth of bold experiments in British Indian Christian worship music due to the influence of secular music.

Sung by the worship group, Mowgli, the popular idiom appeals to the young generation. Here the basic pop group instrumentation is used, a drum set, guitars and keyboards.

Song 14: *Ruh Aah*

> *Chorus:* Come Holy Spirit
>
> 1. When the Holy Spirit comes all shackles are broken
>
> 2. When the Spirit comes, He will purify and clean hearts.

Raj Kaul's music is a combination of his life as a South

Asian brought up in an Afro-Caribbean community; his Christian compositions are in the fusion styles of rap, bhangra, hip-hop and garage, including dance and with Indian lyrics. In *"Kushi Manoa, Let's Rejoice"*, with hip-hop accompaniment, he has composed music to suit his preferred style of singing, although it does not lend itself to assembly singing easily, but indeed does convey the desired theological message.

Song 15*: Kushi Manoa, Let's Rejoice*

Khushi khushi manaao (2)	Come and celebrate now (2)
Bolo bolo Masihaa ki jay, jay, jay (2)	Sing your praises to Jesus with joy, joy joy.

The simplicity of "David's Prayer", performed by the Raja worship group, has proved to be a popular worship song for all to sing. Because of its simplicity and its intended theology it is quickly learnt.

Song 16: *David's Prayer*

Praise be to you O lord my God
You are the holy One.

Yours O lord is the greatness and the power
Yours O Lord is glory and strength

All the earth exalt your name
All heaven glorify your name.

Wealth and honour comes from you
You are the ruler of all things.

In your hands are strength and power
You exalt and give strength to all.

O Lord my God we give you thanks
And praise and glorify your name.

(by Shaji Thomas)

It comes as no surprise that this repertoire has been heavily influenced by popular music, as has liturgical music everywhere. In the simplicity of the songs some measures have been taken to use instruments from India, as well as the dual uses of language. How long this may continue is a matter for speculation. Already it can be noted that a gap has widened between the younger generations of South Asian origin and the older generations who prefer "real" hymns. Even though music may cross cultural barriers, in the Christian community it is acknowledged that the duty to compose lies not only with the composers but also with the congregations who use them. There has also been interaction in a spate of exciting experiments by musicians who are collaborating in playing music from India and from the West[76].

In recent years a reverse mission from Southern and Eastern churches to the churches in the West and North has been notable in the liturgical music of what is termed world or global music. To many who have their origins in the South and East, the addition of the adjectival terms "global" and "world" convey a negative feeling, a feeling of being second class; it is as if their music was worth less than the music from Europe. If Wiora's serious attempt to propose a scheme for the understanding of global music can also be applied to that of music for Christian worship, the question arises about the value of European influence on the music of South Asia, the Caribbean and other former British colonies and Great Britain.

In the first and fourth of these overlapping ages, Wiora envisages a unified musical world. He speculates that in the first

---

76 *One such enterprise, promoted by the Asian Music Circuit, is a series of concerts by Western and Eastern musicians. One presentation has been of two world modal music, Gregorian chant and monophonic songs of the Middle Ages sung by Dominique Vellard, and the classical ragas of North India played on the sarod, a twenty-two stringed lute played by Ken Zuckerman. Other experiments have been on improvisation using jazz and Indian melodic structures (see Gerry Farrell's book).*

age the world was musically homogeneous, as many cultures roughly shared an early history of music. During the next two periods diverging cultures sang and made music appropriate to their social and aesthetic values. In the fourth and final age, or the "global industrial culture", Wiora suggests that all types of music in the world may converge again through forces initially predominant in the West – its technology, economic and political spheres and much more. Following the technological explosion the effect will be the combining of various world cultures in their need to confront Western culture musically[77]. There appears to be a need to syncretise and contextualise indigenous and "foreign" music. No longer is the European way totally valid, as influential changes have emanated from musical forces around the world.

In relation to the *bhajan*-worship song, an attempt to slip many of these devotional songs into the liturgies of the major denominations is obvious. To acknowledge them fully and use them with integrity is a challenge for the churches. Their positions in the liturgy appear as a third or fourth hymn, at the beginning or end of a "normal" service or mass, and as a prayer or meditation. From this it would seem that the perception is one of an unconscious motive, yet cautious attitude, towards conveying a sense of integrated unity among the diversity of mankind. Although this idea is politically new to Western countries, it was an historical factor of survival within the Indian sub-continent, where many external or foreign cultures were embedded within

---

77 *Peter Gabriel, composer, instrumentalist and singer of Genesis, became deeply involved with music of different cultures and established a company called The World of Music, Arts and Dance, better known by its acronym, WOMAD. The first day of the WOMAD festival in 1982 was an educational day when schools were invited to Somerset free of charge; booklets were prepared on topics ranging from Caribbean, Latin American music to Indonesian, African, Indian and British music. Artistes included Ustad Amjad Ali Khan talking about the sarod, and Ustad Imrat Khan about the sitar. This festival has gone from strength to strength and is held at Reading and is known worldwide.*

the local cultures.

The singing of *bhajans* in Christian worship have survived because of the needs and instincts of people who use them. This appeared to die down but there is a revival in Indo-Christian or South Asian communities today. Why? According to a theory of marginal survival by Klass, people who move to a new land tend to preserve their traditions. It could be said that those at home, namely in India, appeared to change their traditions with the times. The *bhajans* sung in Christian worship in the diaspora acted as a stamp of cultural identity. For the first settlers and older immigrants the *bhajan* represented an attachment of communal India to the advent of the New World, being compelled to forget the past yet not negating the present, and having to face the future without choice. Originally it painted a very sad picture of people leaving their old homes and traditions, hoping and wishing for a better life on the morrow. Subsequently, through other generations, the *bhajan* became a badge of cultural identity. Currently, with the flux of new worship songs from around the world, although the form and the music are changing to suit the needs of contemporary generations, the call-and-response model is apparent in conventions for the masses. Like the Taizé repertoire[78], the *bhajan*-worship song repertoire may yet find its niche recognised by the few.

---

78 *The community of Taizé in France was founded by the Swiss Brother Roger (Roger Louis Schutz, 1915-2005), who was a classically trained musician but studied theology at Lausanne. At Taizé he founded an eccumenical order whose religious life was subsumed in music and silence and whose services were candlelit. The music was based on ancient styled mantras which were developed by him and consisted of simple repetitive phrases on which to meditate. Silence was essential and, as Brother Roger said, "with a childlike trust, we let Christ pray silently within us".*

Many older South Asian residents in Europe and America remember some of these *bhajans*, which they used to sing as children and are now published in books like *Songs of Fellowship, Mission Praise* and other contemporary hymnbooks. It has been proposed, in conversation by those who have sung them in childhood, that some of these worship songs have been arranged and termed "anonymous". New styles of the *bhajan* are reflected in the contemporary forms of worship songs which are still recognised by those who sang them in their youth as in the following versions:

Song 17: *Mukti Dil-aye (He saves)*

Peace comes to you in Jesus' name	Mukti di-laaye Yesu naam
Salvation in no other name	Shanti di-laaye Yesu naam
1. Jesus is the Ocean of Grace	Yesu dayaa kaa behtaa saagar
You are the Majestic Lord	Yesu hai daataa mahaan
2. Jesus you were born in a manger	Charni mein tu ne janam liyaa Yesu
You were crucified on the cross	Suli pe kiyaa vishraam
3. For the forgiveness of our sins	Ham sab ke paapon ko mitaane
Jesus has been sacrificed on the cross	Yesu huaa balidaan
4. By shedding your blood on the cross	Krus par apnaa khoon bahaa kar
You paid the full price for our sins	Saaraa chukaayaa daan

(Author unknown, arranged by June George)

Change is inevitable where the recognition of the *bhajan* is concerned. To require modes and forms to remain as "originals" is anathema to development, but the *bhajan* survives in a new dimension as song in Christian worship. Change, which may have been imperceptible at first, is noticeable after a long period of time. Music and form appear not to change unless causes change, and during the interim period changes which occur may be regrettable. The *bhajan* as a devotional song meant identity; it was a testimony in symbol and message; it represented spiritual freedom and was a form of communication and an act of communion between people.

Glossary

Acal	motionless
achut	intangible
Adi Granth	sacred book of the Sikhs
Advaita	philosophical school of absolute monism associated with Sankara
Ahat(e)	audible sound
ahata nada (anahata)	'struck sound', that which is heard
ajnana	to wash away sin
akal	timeless
alamkara	ornamentation in music
Alvars	South Indian composers of hymns
amsa	keynote of a raga, now called the *vadi*
anadi	without any beginning
anahata nada	'unstruck sound', that which is inaudible
anahat	indestructible
a(a)nanda	pure bliss; joy
anil	colourless
anudatta	lower note of a chant
anuvadi	secondary note of a raga
aroha	ascending note pattern
asavari	a thatt/raga; mode/scale
ashram	a place of spiritual retreat and meditation; a community gathered around a holy person
ati-madra	very low bass
ati-tar	very high register
avatar	a descent or incarnation of a god in human form of some other physical body
avroha	descending note pattern
ayoni	unborn

Bedi khatri — merchant caste

bhaj (Sanskrit) — to share in, to give, to belong, to serve God

bhajan — religious song/hymn.

bhakta — devotee to God; worships through icons and images

bhakti — devotion to a god; associated with a movement

bhairavi — scale/mode of E

Bharat — (land of) India

bilava — mode of C

Chamar — worker with hides of dead animals

chit — knowledge

Dadra — six counts in rhythm

dastgahs — Persian modes

Din-I-Ilahi — religion associated with Akbar

drut — fast(tempo)

Dvaita — philosophical school of dualism associated with Madhava

dholak — drum

dhantal — finger cymbals

Ek omkar — Sikh symbol for I OM (om); God is one

ektara — musical instrument

Fakir — Muslim holy man.

Gamak(a)	grace note
gan	to sing verses
ghandaras	family music schools
gopi	milkmaid
graha	starting note of a raga; clef
granti/granthi	reader of Sikh holy scripture
guru	mentor, spiritual teacher
Gurudvara	Sikh temple
Humpitam	appoggiatura (grace note in music)
Ibadat Khana	House of Worship
Jatis	ancient ragas
julaha	weaver
Kafi	mode/raga
kalachepans	(Tamil) song services
kali	rest in music
kalyan	mode/raga
kampita	shake, a musical ornament.
kampita ahata (appoggiatura)	musical ornament
kampita gamaka	ornamental theory in music
kaseeda	Muslim devotional song
keetam	dance drama
khamaj	mode/raga
kirtan	gathering to sing worship songs
kori	weaver
Laud(e)	songs/hymns (of St Francis)
laudesi	Gathering to sing worship songs associated with St Francis
laya	tempo
lina	tonal shadings through glides

Madhya	equivalent to the alto/tenor sounds; middle; medium
Madhyam	moderate tempo
Mahabharata	one of the two great Hindu epics
mantra	a repetitive phrase
mandra	equivalent to the bass sound/voice
maquam	Arabic mode
matra	beat
mela	mode
mida	ripple/slide
Mizah	Thanksgiving prayer
moksha	liberation of the soul from the successive series of births and deaths
Nada	sound
Nam	name (of a deity)
nam bhajan	song in which names of deity were chanted
Nirguna	school of sants who believed God/Brahma to be without form or attributes
niranjal	spotless; without sin
nyasa	last note of raga/cadence
Om	sacred sound
Pakad	phrase by which a raga is recognised
parampara	guru and pupil relationship
phaharas	divisions of the day for worship
puranas	stories about the gods
Quwaali	religious form of Muslim singing in which many voices are heard; an 'utterance' in which the lyrics praise Allah and his prophets
quazi	Muslim learned teacher

Raga	technically, a scale
Raga/Rajah	prince, ruler
ragis	cantors
Raja(h)	Prince, Ruler
Ramayana	one of the two great epics which tells the story of Rama
Rig Veda	the first and most ancient of the Vedic texts
Sabd	the Word in Sikhism
sadhu	Hindu holy man
saguna	devotees who identified with one personal form of God
sahib	term of respect
sam	melody
sama	main beat
samagan	ancient form of chanting in three tones
Samgita	combined song, dance and instrumental style
samvadi	subdominant note of a raga.
sant	someone who is true or good; devotee who worships God without forms
sangeet	that which comprises vocal, instrumental, dance and theatre
sanyasi	an ascetic, hermit
saptak	Indian octave
sargam	sol-fa
Sat	soul's existence, unchangeable
satsang	'truth together'. A gathering to sing and discuss spiritual matters
scrutis	microtones
scruti-patti	pitch box resembling an organ
sthams	registers in music

Sufi	holy man
svaras	seven notes of the scale
svarita	upper note of the scale
Tala (tal)	measure of time in music; rhythmic pattern
tali	minor beat
tar	treble sound
tiripipa-hillola, mordent	music ornament
thatt	a group of ragas.
trimurti	the three forms of supreme reality in relation to the world, relating to Brahma, the Creator, Vishnu the Preserver and Shiva the Destroyer
Udatta	middle note
Upanishad	a set of holy texts of philosophy and religion, the end of the Vedas
Ustad	master (Muslim) of music
Vadi	dominant note of the raga
vali	ripple/slide
vaishnavism	the worship of the god Vishnu
Vedas	Hindu scriptures: the Rig Veda, the Yajar Veda, the Sama Veda, the Atharva Vedas; also the Brahamas and the Upanishads
Vedanta	end of the Vedas
vibhag	a group of beats; a bar
vilambit	slow tempo
vinaya	petition
Vishishtadvaita	school of modified monism associated with Ramanuja
Yogi	wiseman

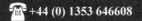

MELROSE BOOKS
TITLE ORDER FORM

ORDERING

☎ **CALL** +44 (0) 1353 646608

💻 **INTERNET**
www.melrosebooks.com

✉ **POST**
Melrose Books
St Thomas Place
Ely, Cambridgeshire
CB7 4GG, UK

🗎 **FAX**
+44 (0) 1353 646602

@ **EMAIL**
sales@melrosebooks.com

QUANTITY	TITLE	ISBN	PRICE	TOTAL
	The Bhajan - Christian Devotional Music in the Indian Diaspora	978-1-906050-51-1	£12.99	

POSTAGE RATES		
UK	£2.30 per book	plus 90p for each additional copy
Europe	£3.90 per book	plus £1.70 for each additional copy
USA / Rest of the World	£6.55	plus £3.60 for each additional copy

POSTAGE £ / $ ___ : ___

GRAND TOTAL £ ___ : ___

PERSONAL DETAILS

TITLE   SURNAME   FIRST NAME

ORGANISATION

ADDRESS

COUNTRY   TEL

FAX   EMAIL

PAYMENT DETAILS

SELECT PAYMENT METHOD

☐ **CHEQUE** payable to Melrose Books for the amount of ___ : ___

(For international convenience all credit card charges will be made in Sterling)

CREDIT CARD ☐ **VISA** ☐ **AMEX** ☐ **MASTERCARD** ☐ **SWITCH**   **ISSUE NO** *(IF SHOWN)* ☐

3 digit Card security No.

START DATE
(SWITCH ONLY) ☐☐ / ☐☐

SIGNATURE

DATE ___ / ___ / ___

EXPIRY DATE ☐☐ / ☐☐

PLEASE KEEP ME INFORMED OF ALL NEW TITLES BY MELROSE BOOKS:

BY POST ☐   BY EMAIL ___

PLEASE KEEP ME INFORMED OF NEW TITLES IN ONLY THIS GENRE BY MELROSE BOOKS:

BY POST ☐   BY EMAIL ___

Bibliography and List of Sources

Allchin, Raymond (1964), *Tulsi Das, Kavitavali* (translated), London: George Allen & Unwin

Appasamy, A. (1966), *Tamil Christian Poet (The life and Writings of H. A. Krishna Pillai),* London: Lutterworth Press

Archbishops' Commission on Church Music (Report) (1992), *In Tune with Heaven*, London: Church House Publishing; Hodder & Stoughton

Armstrong, Karen (2007), *The Great Transformation, The Beginning of Our Religious Traditions*, Toronto: Vintage Canada

Bake, Dr Arnold (1957), The Music of India.' In Egon Wellesz (ed.), *New Oxford History of Music*, 1, Ancient and Oriental London: OUP, Vol.1, pages 195-227

Barbiracki, Carol M. (1985) 'Indigenizers', In: Nettl, Bruno (ed) *The Western Impact on World Music (Change, Adaptation, and Survival)*, London: Collier Macmillan Publishers, pages 96-100

Best, F. Thomas Helbr Dagmar, editors (1995) *So We Believe, So We Pray* (Towards Koinonia in Worship), Geneva: World Council of Churches

Bharop, Anil (30 June 2007) *Integration and the real balance of Power*, London: The Sunday Times

Birbalsingh, Frank, editor (1988) *Bahaji Bhai (an anthology of Indo-Caribbean Literature)*, Toronto: TSAR

Boyd, Robin, (1969) *An Introduction to Indian Christian Theology*, Madras: The Christian Literature Society

Box, Reginald (1996) *Make Music to Our God - How We Sing the Psalms*, England: SPCK

Brown, Leslie (1956) [1982], *The Indian Christians of St Thomas - An Account of the Ancient Syrian Church of Malabar*, England: Cambridge University Press

Carmichael, Amy, *H.A. Krishna Pillai*

Carroll, David, editor (1972) *The Taj Mahal*, London: The Reader's Digest Ass. Ltd

Clayton, Martin (2001) *Time in Indian Music* (Rhythm, Metre and Form in North Indian Rag Performance), England: OUP

Cowley, John (1996) *Carnival Canboulay and Calypso* (Traditions in the Making) England: Cambridge University Press

Cross, Malcolm (1972), The East Indians of Guyana and Trinidad, Minority Rights Group Report No. 13, England

Danielou, Alain (1968) *The Ragas of North Indian Music,* GB: Barrie and Rocklift

Davie, Grace (1994) *Religion in Britain since 1945,* UK: Blackwell

Davis, Merle J. (1942) thesis, *The East Indian Church in Trinidad*, Report of a survey, Trinidad: St Andrew's Theological College

Davison, T. Archibald and Apel, Willi, (1946, 1949), *Historical Anthology of Music Volume 1, Oriental, Medieval and Renaissance Music,* USA; Harvard University Press

Duchesneau, Claude and Veuthey, Michel (translated by Paul Inwood) (1992) *Music and Liturgy*, Washington: The Pastoral Press

Duncan, Stephen, (August 1991), *A Study of the uses of Indigenous Music in the Rites of the Roman Catholic Church on the Subcontinent of India since the Second Vatican Council with particular attention to Bhajan and Kirtan,* USA: Memphis State University

—— (1999) *A Genre in Hindusthani Music (Bhajans) as Used in the Roman Catholic Church,* United Kingdom: The Edward Mellon Press Ltd.

Farrell, Gerry (1997) *Indian Music in the West,* England: OUP

Farquhar, J.N. (1920) *Outline of the Religious Literature of India,* London: OUP:

Flannery, Austin, editor (1988 revised) *Vatican Council 11 The Conciliar and Post Conciliar Documents* New York: Costello Publishing Co.

Foley, Edward (1995) *Studies in Liturgical Musicology*, USA: The Pastoral Press

Gallagher, Joseph, editor (1966) *The Constitution on the Sacred Liturgy* (English Translation), The Documents of Vatican II, New York: Guild Press

Garcia, A. (1969) *History of the West Indies*, England: Harrap and Co. Ltd,

Garrett, T.S. (1958) *Worship in the Church of South India* London: Lutterworth Press

Gidoomal, Ram & Thomson, Robin (1997) *A Way of Life*, GB: Hodder and Stoughton

Gidoomal, R. & Fearon, M. (1994) *Karma n. Chips,* England: Wimbledon Publishing Co.

Glass, Philip (1988) *Opera on the Beach: Philip Glass on His New World of Theatre Music,* London: Faber & Faber

Hale, Christopher Dicran (2000) thesis, *Christian Bhajans - A Survey of their Use in the North Indian Hindi Belt and their Critique by Hindu Professional Musicians in the Indian World,* Briercrest Biblical Seminary, Saskatchewan, Canada

Harman, Alec (1958) *Mediaeval and Early Renaissance Music (up to c. 1525),* London: Rockliff

Hastings, A. (1986) *A History of English Christianity 1929-1985,* London: Collins

Hawley, John Stratton and Juergensmeyer, Mark (1988) *Songs of the Saints of India* New York: Oxford University Press INC

Hayburn F. Robert (1979) Papal Legislation on Sacred Music: 95AD to 1977 AD, Colegeville: The Liturgical Press.

Holeton, R. editor (1990) *Liturgical Inculturation in the Anglican Communion,* (Alcuin/GROW Liturgical Study 15) Nottingham: Grove Books Ltd.

Holroyd, Peggy (1972) *Indian Music - A Vast Ocean of Promises,* GB: George Allen & Unwin Ltd

Hughes, Anslem Dom, (1966) *Plainsong for English Choirs,* Great Britain: The Faith Press Ltd

Jacobs, Arthur (1972) *A Short History of Western Music,* Britain: Penguin

Jairazbhoy, N. A. (1971) *The Rags of North Indian Music - Their Structure & Evolution,* London: Faber and Faber

Jenni, Martin, (1996) "Ancient Sacred Monody - The Western Parallel", In: Madras Music Journal, Volume LXVII, India

Karolyi, Otto (1998) "The Indian Subcontinent" in: *Traditional African and Oriental Music,* London: Penguin, pages 97-142

Kartomi, Margaret and McCredie, Andrew D (June 2004) *Musical Outcomes of Jewish Migration into Asia via the Northern and Southern Routes c 1780-1950* in Ethnomusicology Forum 13/1 Silk, Spice and Shirah, Oxford: Taylor & Francis Ltd

Keay, John (1981), *India Discovered*, England: Windward

Klass, Morton (1961) *East Indians in Trinidad (A Study of Cultural Persistence)*, New York: Columbia University Press

Kuckerty, J. editor (1976) *Indian Music in Divine Service* in Musica Indigena, Rome

Lott, E. J. editor (1986) *Worship in an Indian Context,* Bangalore: United Theological College.

Macnicol, Nicol (1919) *Psalms of Marathna Saints: 108 Hymns*, translated from the Marathi, Calcutta: Oxford University Press

Macnicol, Nicol (1930) *India in the Dark Wood,* London: The Cargate Press

Mammen, A. T. Rev. (n.d.) Mar Thoma Syrian Church of Malabar

Manasseh, Sara (June 2004) *Religious Music Traditions of the Jewish-Babylonian Diaspora in Bombay* in Ethnomusicology Forum (Silk, Spice and Shirah) Volume 13 (1), Oxford: Taylor & Francis Ltd

Massey, Reginald & Jamila (1993) *The Music of India*, London: Khan & Averill

McEvilley, Thomas (2002) *The Shape of Ancient Thought - Comparative Studies in Greek and Indian Philosophies*, New York: Allworth Press

McKinnon, James, editor (1987) *Music in Early Christian Literature*, England: Cambridge University Press

Merriam, Alan P. (1955) *The Use of Music in the Study of a Problem of Acculturation* in American Anthropologist Number 57, pp28-33

Milton, Giles (1999) *Nathaniel's Nutmeg*, London: Hodder & Stoughton

Myers, Helen (1978) "The Process of Change in Trinidad East Indian Music," In *Journal of the Indian Sociological Society*, Volume 9, Number 3, pages 12-16 (Source: Nettl 1985)

—— (1993) editor *The New Grove Handbooks, Ethnomusicology - Historical and Regional Studies*, UK: The Macmillan Press Ltd

—— (1998) *Music of Hindu Trinidad*, Chicago: University of Chicago Press

Neehall, R.G, (1958) Presbyterianism in Trinidad, New York City: United Theological Seminary.

Neill, Stephen (1961) Christian Faith and Other Faiths, (The Christian Dialogue with other Religions) London, Oxford University Press

—— (1970) *The Story of the Christian Church in India and Pakistan,* USA: William B. Eerdmans Publishing Co.

Nettl, Bruno & Bohlman, Philip V, editors (1991) *Comparative Musicology and Anthropology of Music (Essays on the History of Musicology)*, USA: The University of Chicago Press

Newbigin, Lesslie (1989), The Gospel in a Pluralist Society, Great Britain: SPCK

Parthasarathy, T.S, editor *Madras Music Journal*, Volume LXVII pages 89-92 India: Madras Music Academy

Patasar, Sharda, (2000) *Indian Music in a New World Context: Identity in Indo-Trinidadian Music*, Trinidad & Tobago: University of the West Indies

Paul, Rajaiah D. (1952) *The Cross over India,* London: SCM Press

Popley, H.A. (1921a) *The Music of India,* Madras: Oxford University Press.

—— (1990 reprinted) *The Music of India,* Delhi: OUP

Prabhakar, Samson (1995) The Church of South India Liturgy of the Eucharist, in *So We Believe, So We Pray* Geneva: World Council of Churches

Ramlakhan, K. editor (1994) *SMARANA* - A Collection of Traditional Bhajans in Hindi and English, Trinidad: Dev Naagri Publishers

Ramnarine, Tina (1998) *"Brotherhood of the Boat": musical dialogues in a Caribbean context,* in British Journal of Ethnomusicology Volume 7, Sheffield

Ramsaran, John A. (1973) *English and Hindi Religious Poetry An Analogical Study,* Leiden: EJ Brill

Rao, Subba T.V. (1962) *Studies in Indian Music,* India: Asia Publishing House

Ravikumar, Geetha (1996) "Bhajan Singing Style in Hindusthani Music", In: T.S. Parthasarathy, (Editor) *Journal of the Music Academy*, Volume LXVII, pages 187-192 India: Madras Music Academy

Reich, Steve (1974) *Writings about Music*, Halifax, Nova Scotia

Robertson, Alec and Stevens, Denis, editors (1960, reprinted 1966) *The Pelican History of Music, Volume 1*, London: Penguin Books Limited

Root, John (1998) "Aims for Ministry in a multi-faith Community" In: Shivdanasi, S. & Niles, A. (editors) *Asian Opportunity* United Kingdom: South Asian Concern

Sachs, Curt (1963) *A Short History World Music*, London: Dennis Dobson 2nd edition

Sadie, Stanley, editor (1984) *The Grove Dictionary of Musical Instruments* Volumes 1 & 2, London: Macmillan Press Ltd

Samaroo, B. (1987) "Two Abolitions: African Slavery and East Indian Indentureship" In: Dabydeen, D. & Samaroo, B. (editors), *India in the Caribbean,* London: Hansib Publishing Limited, pages 25-56

Samaroo, Brinsley, editor (1996) *Pioneer Presbyterians*, (Origins of Presbyterian work in Trinidad), Institute of Caribbean Studies: Trinidad

Samaroo, Brinsley (2000) *The Caribbean Consequences of the Indian Revolt of 1857*, Trinidad & Tobago: University of the West Indies

Sastri, B.V.K. (1973) "Nijaguna Sivayogi," In: T.S.Parthasarathy, (editor) *Journal of the Music Academy* Madras Volume XLIV, pages 202-222 India: Madras Music Academy

Scarf, Christopher Hans (May 1999 thesis) *Psalms: Form or Function? - Fulfilled in the Music of the Synagogue - And in the Transfer of the Psalter to the Early Church*, England: Colchester Institute (Anglia Polytechnic University)

Sen, Amartya (2005) *The Argumentative Indian - Writings on Indian History, Culture and Identity*, England: Allen Lane (Penguin Books)

Shivdanasi, S. & Niles, A. (1998) *Asian Opportunity,* England: South Asian Concern,

Soares, M. and Bhupsingh, H. (1988) *Celebration- A Centenary History of Aramalaya Presbyterian Church* 1881-1981 Trinidad

Strangways, A.H. Fox (1914) *The Music of Hindostan,* GB: O.U.P

Sutcliffe, Sally J. (1998) *Good News for Asians in Britain,* Cambridge: Grove Books Limited

Tagore, Rabindranath (1988 reissued) *The Religion of Man* Great Britain: Cox & Wyman

The Bible - Revised Standard Version (1952) GB: William Collins Son & Co. Ltd

Thomson, Robin (1998) "Looking for Lessons" In: Shivdanasi, S, & Niles, A, (editors) *Asian Opportunity,* United Kingdom: South Asian Concern

The Times Atlas of World History (1978) Times Books, London

The Times Atlas of Medieval Civilizations, (1990) Times Books London

Tinker, H. (1973) *A New System of Slavery*, London

Vertovec Steven, (1992) Hindu Trinidad: Religion, Ethnicity and Socio-Economic Change, London: Macmillan, Warwick University Press.

de Verteuil, Anthony (1989) *Eight East Indian Immigrants,* Paria Publishing Co. Ltd: Port-of-Spain, Trinidad

Visram, Rozina (1993) South Asians in London, In: Nick Merriman (editor), *The Peopling of London (Fifteen Thousand Years of Settlement from Overseas)*, GB: The Museum of London, pages 169-177

Wardell, Margaret & Gidoomal, R. (1994) *Chapatis for Tea*, England: Highland Books

White, Eammon E. (1971) *Appreciating India's Music* Boston: Crescendo Publishing Co.

Widdess, Richard (1995) *The Ragas of Early Indian Music (Modes, melodies and musical notations from the Gupta period to c.1250),* England: Clarendon Press

Williams, Eric (1964) *History of the People of Trinidad and Tobago* Great Britain: Andre Deutsch

Winter, Miriam Theresa (1984) *Why Sing? Towards a Theology of Catholic Church Music*, USA: Pastoral Press

Wiora, Walter (1965) *The Four Ages of Music*, New York: Norton

Wood, Josephine (2000) *Songs of Everlasting Praise: Ostinato from Songs of Taize and their Value for common Worship* - dissertation

Woodfield, Ian (1994) "Collecting Indian Songs in late eighteenth century Lucknow: Problems of Transmission, In: Widdess R (Editor) *British Journal of Ethnomusicology*, Volume 3 pages 76-96, London: International Council for Traditional Music, UK Chapter

Unpublished Sources

Call Me Trishanku by J Ansuman Ramsaran (A Self Study)

Letters and Papers by Leslie C Sankarsingh

Music Collections

2003 *Aaraadhanaa ho* Satya Bhavan Sutton: South Asian Concern

1988 *Caribbean Hymnal,* England: House of McCrimmon

Ferguson, Howard, editor, *Early English Keyboard Music* Oxford: OUP

Davison, Archibald T. and Apel, Willi, *Historical Anthology of Music, England: Oxford*

Jewels in His Crown - Song book 1999 Kirpa Culture

Kirpa Ke Geet - Collection of songs for multi-cultural Worship: Kirpa Culture Leicester

Thomson, David M. (1991) *Rejoice and Sing*, England: Oxford University Press

Songs of Fellowship 2 (1999) Great Britain: Kingsway Communications Ltd.

Chauharjasingh, Archibald (1991) *Bhajans of the Early Presbyterian Church* Private Collection

Kowlessar, Edward (n.d.) *Christian Bhajans*

Lazarus, Vijay and Stephenson, Muriel J. (editors), *Aradhna Ke Git (Fijian Hymns)*

Marshall-Taylor, Geoffrey (1988) *Come and Praise 2* London: BBC Enterprises Ltd

Articles
(newspapers and magazines)

CONCERN October 1999, January 2007

Gledhill, Ruth, *Let us pray* - in Urdu 6/5/2000 *The Weekend Times*

Sunday Guardian 30/5/1999 (a) Christian Indians from India

—— (b) Christian Heritage

—— (c) Indian Arrival Day Trinidad: Trinidad Publishing Co. Ltd.

Sieunarine, Everson T, "A Cloud of Witnesses, God's Servant" in: *The Trinidad Presbyterian*, November 1990 Trinidad: The Presbyterian Church of Trinidad & Tobago

Gopaul, Winston B, "Saris and Shalwars adorn Susamachar" July 1995 in: *The Trinidad Presbyterian*, (July 1995), Trinidad: The Presbyterian Church of Trinidad & Tobago

"Discoveries for 1992" In: *The Trinidad Presbyterian* (ibid)

www.cidern.arnd.edu/inscr/mar/assessment
www. adb.online.anu.edu.au/biogs

Index

Note

Page numbers in bold are for glossary terms, e.g. Mahabharata   45(Fig. 3), 46(Fig. 4), 48, 49, **142**

Page numbers followed by (ex.) are for examples of songs, e.g. Bilaval Thatt   72, 90(ex. 3)

Page numbers followed by (Fig.) are for figures, e.g. Mahabharata   45(Fig. 3)

Page numbers followed by (n) are for footnotes, e.g. thatt(s)   52, 71–2, 90, 91(n.54)

Page numbers in italics are for illustrations, e.g. bamboo flute   *123*

A

B

Boyd, Robin   80, 82, 83
Brahamas   47
Brahmins   34
Britain *see* Anglican Church; Great Britain
Brown, Bishop Leslie   59, 84
Brown, Hilary, *I Am / Main Haan* (song 11)   129–30
Buddhism, in India   xv, 5
Burgess, Francis   94
Burton, John Wear, *Fiji of Today* (1910)   6

C

call-and-response   38–40, 75, 93, 96–7
   in contemporary music   128, 132
   and direct repetition   104–10
   and Litany patterns   110–13
Canadian Presbyterian Church, West Indies   xiv, 8–9, 11–12, 15
cantus firmus   92
caste   27
Catholic Church *see* Roman Catholic Church
chac-chacs   118
chamar   26–7, **140**
chanting/chants
   plainsong   92, 94
   Samagan   50–1
   syncretism of European and Hindu   69–70, 93, 94
chit (knowledge)   78, **140**
chordal harmony   98, 103
chords
   tetrachords in *Saman* chant   51, 53
   used a drones   98
Christ *see* God; Jesus
Christayan (Tilak)   81–3

Christian *bhajan* see *bhajan*
Christian *Bhakti*   76–85
Christian liturgy   1–4, 44, 88, 89
  see also orders of service; worship
Christian lyrics   76–85
Christianity
  development of ritual and music in   44, 125–8
  East Indian converts to   10–12
  Hindu and Christian saints compared   32
  and Hinduism, compared   31
  in India   14–15, 58–68
  influence on Hinduism   47–8
  see also Anglican Church; Church in India; Indian Christians;
    missionaries; Presbyterian Church; Roman Catholic Church
Church in India
  history of   58–68
  Western influences in   4, 5, 68
  see also Christianity; Indian Christians
Church Missionary Society (CMS)   6, 63
churches, used by Asian Christians in UK   19
clapping   116
community singing *see kirtan(a)*
consonance   54, 55
  samvadi (consonant note)   50, 52, **143**
contemporary music   22, 67, 68, 98–9, 125–9
counterpoint   92
cue signal   106–7
cultural identity   3, 10, 20, 116
culture
  East Indian   xiv–xv, 14
  Indian   xv, 42–3, 44, 49(Fig. 5), 70, 114
  South Asian, in UK   20–1
  Western   19, 48
  see also acculturation; Christianity

D

E

East Indians   xiv–xv, 6, 8–12, 113, 126
   see also Trinidad and Tobago; West Indies
ek omkar (I OM *or* OM)   29, **140**
ektara   **140**
ending note (*nyasa*)   52, **142**
Epics, Hindu   48
Europe
   Christian South Asians in   21, 113
   colonies in India   68
   colonies in West Indies   68
existence (*Sat*)   78, **143**

F

fakir   25, **140**
Farrell, Gerry   75
Fatephur Sikri, *Ibadat Khana*   65
Fekete, Chris and Doug, *All Good Gifts – Uske nam* (song 12)
   130–1
fifth (interval of)   54, 98
Fiji   6
finger cymbals   114
Foley, Edward   43
Fountain of Love (solo) (song 8)   108
fourth (interval of)   51, 54, 98
Fowkes, Margaret   73
fundamental note (tonic)   91, 98, 125
funerals   13–14

G

K

keyboard instruments   73, 118
khajri   117
khamaj   72, 90, **141**
kirtan(a)   25, 37–8, 79, 104–5, 106, **141**
knowledge (*chit*)   78, **140**
kori   27–8, **141**
Kottayam, CMS College in   63
Krishna   24, 31–2, 33
Kushi Manoa, Let's Rejoice (Kaul) (song 15)   133

L

language *see* Hindi; Punjabi; Sanskrit; Syriac; vernacular
   languages
laude   38, **141**
laya   103, **141**
learning, music   44, 104, 107, 108
Leicester   20–1
lina   94, **141**
Litany pattern   110–13 (Figs 12 and 13)
liturgy *see* Christian liturgy; orders of service
lota   118
lower note (*anudatta*)   51, **139**
lyrics
   of Christian *bhajans*   127–8
   of Christian *Bhakti*   76–85
   of Hindu *bhajans*   24

M

N

O

S

U

V

W

X

Y